Starting a Nonprofit

by Ann Fritschner

BARNES & NOBLE BOOKS

NEW YORK

D1413717

While Barnes & Noble and the author have used best efforts in writing this book, they make no representations or warranties as to its accuracy and completeness. It is sold with the understanding that neither the author nor Barnes & Noble are engaged in rendering legal, accounting, or other professional service. If legal advice or other expert assistance is required, the services of a competent professional person should be sought.

© 2006 by Barnes & Noble Publishing, Inc.

All rights reserved. No part of this book may be used or reproduced in any manner whatsoever without the written permission of the Publisher.

FIRST EDITION

© 2006 Barnes & Noble Books

Barnes & Noble Publishing
122 Fifth Avenue
New York, NY 10011

ISBN 0760773912

2 4 6 8 10 9 7 5 3 1

Printed and bound in the United States of America.

introduction

"We worked hard and it showed: Our project was growing by leaps and bounds. Even without a nonprofit sponsor we were raising more than enough money to keep our program going! And then it dawned on us—why don't we convert our project into a nonprofit organization? So I took on the task of finding out how to do just that. I read what I could, but everything was very technical. The more I researched the process, the more complicated it seemed. Who knew the nonprofit world was so big and unwieldy?"

Who indeed? Enter **Barnes & Noble Business Basics** *Starting a Nonprofit*. It not only explains how the nonprofit world works, but also shows you how to start and operate your own nonprofit. All you need to know is here: how to define your mission, apply for tax-exempt status from the IRS, balance your books, organize volunteers, find funding, throw a special fundraising event, write a successful grant, and much more. So read on and get the inside scoop on how to start and run a nonprofit. Your nonprofit is out there waiting to come into its own—starting it just became a whole lot easier.

Barb Chintz
Editorial Director, the **Barnes & Noble Business Basics**™ series

table of contents

1
Starting out

starting a nonprofit

Giving your good idea room to grow

Your idea for a charity project has taken off and is growing by leaps and bounds. A number of people have joined to help you in your cause. In fact, together you have raised enough money to fund it, and you are fairly certain that you want to keep the project going. Good for you! This is terrific. But often this kind of success can create its own problems. How so? Well, you will have to pay taxes on any money you've raised for your charitable project that you can't expense or don't spend.

Moreover, as your project grows, you may find yourself stretched thin. You may need a dedicated phone line, more-professional publicity campaigns about your next key events, and perhaps some paid administrative help to handle all the work of running your nonprofit.

What should you do? You have several options.
1. Continue on with your good works and do nothing. Keep your project simple and don't expand it.

2. Find an existing nonprofit that wants to take over your program and serve your clients (see page 18).

3. Start your own nonprofit business. Here you turn your project into a public business, giving it a legal structure. There are a lot of good reasons to do this. By making your nonprofit a separate legal business, you and your co-volunteers are shielded somewhat from liabilities, such as lawsuits or debts your nonprofit may incur. And by becoming a formal business you will get an EIN (employer identification number) that will allow your nonprofit to have its own bank account and own property. If your nonprofit business has more than $25,000 in gross receipts, your next step should be to file for tax-exempt status with the IRS.

ASK THE EXPERTS

How do I know if I am the type of person to start a nonprofit?

Think about how you approach problems on the job or at home. Consider how you approach your current job or jobs you had in the past. If you are an independent thinker, like to solve problems, can plan ahead, and are not averse to taking a few risks, chances are you are more than capable of starting a nonprofit. Most nonprofit owners are energetic people who are passionate about their work and persevere in the face of setbacks. Here are some of the main reasons people start nonprofits:

- You find helping others to be a very meaningful way to live.

- You have a passion about a cause that will help make the world a better place.

- You are willing to take risks and try new methods to solve old problems.

I already have a for-profit business, but I want to start a nonprofit to market a creative toy I have invented for children with disabilities. Can I do that?

Sure. A lot of nonprofits start as an adjunct to for-profit businesses. If you have a local business, starting a nonprofit business is a great way to give back to your community. You need to be very careful about making sure that the two businesses are kept separate from each other and that those who work in your for-profit business have no conflict of interest with your nonprofit business. You can also consider creating a foundation instead of a nonprofit corporation. With a foundation you can receive tax-exempt funds from your for-profit business and distribute them to charitable causes. (For more on starting a foundation, see pages 12–15.)

profit vs. nonprofit

What are the differences?

A nonprofit business has just enough things in common with a for-profit business to cause a lot of confusion. After all, both are businesses. However, the purpose of a nonprofit is charity, while the purpose of a for-profit business is just that—profit. Because charitable work is so valued by our society, however, its success has been greatly encouraged by legislators. In fact, when the federal

FOR-PROFIT BUSINESSES

- **Purpose:** profit for the owner.

- **Ownership:** individual owner, partners, or shareholders.

- **Business planning:** business plan, projected budgets, marketing plans.

- **Means of raising money:** loans from banks or private investors, selling shares in the company.

- **Sources of revenues:** selling products or services.

- **Legal structure:** sole proprietorship, partnership, limited liability company (LLC), corporation—here the business is owned by its shareholders and called a C Corp.

- **Taxes:** pays federal, state, and city income taxes as well as sales taxes. Pays employment taxes on staff. Also pays property taxes.

- **Distribution of profits:** Profits are distributed to the owners (partners or shareholders), often in the form of dividends or a year-end distribution of profits.

- **Dissolution or liquidation:** If the business is dissolved, the assets of the business (including accumulated earnings) are distributed to the owners in proportion to their ownership interest.

income tax act was made law in 1894, there was an exemption for those businesses or organizations that were formed solely for charitable, religious, or educational purposes. That exemption continues to this day. There are many other ways in which nonprofits and for-profits differ. To clear some of the misunderstandings, here is a chart:

NONPROFIT BUSINESSES

- **Purpose:** charitable, religious, or educational.

- **Ownership:** the public (sometimes referred to as a community trust). Yes, you and your board members may start a nonprofit, but the public owns it, not you or your board. There are no outright owners. (Nor can there be any conflict of interests within a non-profit; for example, a board member being awarded a contract from a nonprofit for which she is also a volunteer.)

- **Business planning:** business plan, projected budgets, marketing plans.

- **Means of raising money:** fundraising, such as mail solicitations; loans from banks.

- **Sources of revenues:** donations from the public; grant money from the government or private foundations; selling products or services to a charitably inclined group of individuals, such as a college, hospital, or nursing home.

- **Legal structure:** A nonprofit can never be a sole proprietorship. Depending on state law, it can be a corporation, a limited liability corporation, or a trust.

- **Taxes:** pays employment taxes on staff; if it has been granted IRS tax exemption, it is exempt from federal income taxes, and depending on state laws, it is exempt from state and city taxes, sales taxes, and property taxes.

- **Distribution of surplus:** If the nonprofit has earnings in excess of expenses (which is permissible for a nonprofit), the surplus must be used to further charitable purposes. It can also be retained as a reserve in case of a charitable need in the future.

- **Dissolution or liquidation:** If a nonprofit is dissolved or liquidated, all of its assets or retained earnings must be distributed to another charity or the state or the federal government.

the nonprofit world

Nonprofits (also called agencies, organizations, or foundations) come in all shapes and sizes. Some are all about serving the needy, while others provide funding for social groups, such as your local garden club or a labor union. Still others exist to help for-profit businesses stay in business, such as the chamber of commerce. In fact, the world of nonprofits is huge. Nonprofits are currently responsible for 2% of the gross national product, and they are now the fastest-growing sector in the U. S. economy.

The IRS recognizes different types or categories of nonprofits, depending on their purpose and whom they serve and how. In general, the nonprofit world is divided up accordingly.

Public nonprofits: The money to fund these nonprofits comes from the public whom they serve. These services can be educational, cultural, community service, even advocacy services. The United Way and the Red Cross are public nonprofits. Chances are your nonprofit will fall into this category.

Private foundations: Here a nonprofit is formed for the sole purpose of giving money to other charities or other nonprofits. A foundation has a limited or single private source of funding. There are large foundations, such as the Rockefeller Foundation, that give away millions of dollars annually, as well as small family-run foundations that give away less than $5,000 annually.

Membership-supported nonprofits: What sets these nonprofits apart from others is that they are supported by their members, not the public. For example, garden clubs, labor unions, college fraternities, and environmental groups are member-supported nonprofits.

Service nonprofits: These organizations provide services to the public; for example, hospitals and schools.

ASK THE EXPERTS

I want to start a nonprofit so I can get grant money to help out our local theater. How can I do that?

In order to apply for a grant (be it from the government or a private foundation), your nonprofit will need to have tax-exempt status. Only those nonprofits that have applied and been granted IRS tax exemption can apply for grant money.

I inherited money from a family trust, and I want to start a nonprofit to give some of it away. How does that work?

The IRS has a nonprofit for this. It is called a private foundation. Private foundations get most of their financial support from an endowment or large gifts from a family or small group. Public charities, on the other hand, must get at least one-third of their money from the public. (For more on this public support test, see page 92.) To avoid abuses of the tax exemptions, the IRS requires more reporting from private foundations than from public charities.

I heard nonprofits referred to as the independent sector. What is that?

It is the language of the economists. The private sector is where businesses make a profit for their owners or shareholders. The public sector is the part of our economy that deals with goods and services that benefit the public good, usually associated with governments; for example, the police force, the mail service, road repair crews, jails, and prison services. The independent sector is the part of our economy that provides goods and services usually at below-market cost; these services are better known as charitable or philanthropic activities.

planning it

What's involved in starting a nonprofit?

There is a lot of effort involved in starting a nonprofit. Here are the major phases you will need to work through:

The first is called the **idea research phase**. This is where you test your idea for a nonprofit business by doing research to find out how viable your idea really is. Is there a need for your nonprofit service or product? If the need is there and is not being effectively met by other nonprofits or for-profit businesses, find out why. How will your idea solve the problem?

Next comes the people phase. You will need to gather **like-minded people** to help you start your nonprofit. These people will become your future board of directors and volunteers.

How do you want to **structure** your nonprofit business? Do you want to stay small? Do you want legal protection from liabilities? Do you want to be able to apply for grants and other tax-exempt money? How big or small do you want to be?

Once all these questions are answered, you are ready for some hard-core planning in the form of a **business plan**. This is where you map out the details of your nonprofit, including all your financial information.

With all that out of the way, it's time to think about a **publicity campaign** (to get the word out about your service) and a **fund-raising campaign** (to raise money so you can stay in business).

The last phase you need to plan for is the ongoing success of your business. This means planning for **growth** and keeping an eye out for possible pitfalls.

Okay so far? Good. You have been in the big picture phase; now it's time for the details.

ASK THE EXPERTS

Why do nonprofits fail?

For many nonprofits, it is not a question of success or failure; rather some nonprofits simply fizzle out. There are many reasons for this, the biggest one being lack of planning. Like for-profit businesses, nonprofits need a **business plan**—a financial plan that ensures that they are raising enough money to cover their expenses. More than that, nonprofits need a funding plan to help sustain their growth. Other reasons for failure are not keeping good records, failing to comply with state laws about nonprofits, and not keeping IRS-compliant for tax-exempt status.

FIRST PERSON INSIGHTS

It's about the work, not me.

I had a strong interest in helping the homeless; in fact, it was almost a calling. One day I got the chance to help out at my church's shelter. From there, I started a small volunteer project to help neighbors with housing trouble in my town. As my project grew, I got a great group of people together to help but I found they kept turning to me to answer every question. I realized that if this continued, the project would be totally about me and not the work. I decided to turn the project into a nonprofit business and create an official board of directors. I split my job into several parts and asked different people to take them over. That helped enormously and made the project that much richer for the new perspectives. Becoming a nonprofit not only got us tax-exempt status, but it also ensured our long-term success. **—Aaron K., Danbury, CT**

incorporating or not

The big decision

The decision to structure your nonprofit formally as a nonprofit corporation is a big one. For starters, no one starts a nonprofit corporation by himself. You will need to gather a group of like-minded folks who can help you write up your nonprofit's purpose, or **mission,** as well as hammer out and write up **articles of incorporation** (the legal description of your nonprofit and how it will be run). A few of your group of like-minded souls will become members of your board of directors. They will then work with you to write your nonprofit's **bylaws** (specific rules about how your board will operate; for example, specifying how long board members will serve). You will no doubt need to consider buying liability insurance for your nonprofit.

If you want to apply for tax exemption, then you *must* be a corporation, a limited liability company, or a trust. (For more on this, see pages 86–89.) The basic definition of a tax-exempt 501(c)(3) nonprofit organization is one that serves the public good and is organized and operated for religious, charitable, or educational purposes. (It's a good idea to check with other nonprofits that do work similar to yours to make sure your idea really does fall into the tax-exempt nonprofit world.) The IRS will also require a three-year budget for a nonprofit business. (Don't panic, you can do it. For more on that, see page 90.) You will also have to appoint someone to keep detailed financial records of your nonprofit's business and file annual tax returns.

Yes, this does all come down to a lot of work, but with planning, it is much easier. Incorporating is often the only way to really launch a nonprofit idea and ensure you can do the most good with it.

Nonprofit Professional Help

If the decision seems overwhelming, stop and take a deep breath. You are not alone in feeling butterflies at the thought of incorporating your project into a nonprofit. Before you dive in, take some time and do a little research. Start by contacting other nonprofits (local chapters of national ones as well as independent ones) that do work similar to that of your nonprofit. (Remember, there is little competition in the nonprofit world for customers, only for fundraising dollars.) For instance, if you want to run an after-school program for disadvantaged kids, contact those nonprofits that serve a similar community in your state and ask how they got started and how they are managing.

Next go online and start reading about nonprofits and how they work. There are a number of key Web sites devoted to the nonprofit world that can help answer your questions. Start with the National Council of Nonprofit Associations at **www.ncna.org**. Next check out the various search engines on the Internet for information about starting a nonprofit.

Nonprofit lawyers. At some point in your decision making about incorporating, it is helpful to contact a nonprofit lawyer. A nonprofit lawyer can do as much or as little as you need. She can answer your legal questions, review your incorporation papers, or do everything from drawing up your incorporation papers to filing your IRS tax-exempt forms. To find a nonprofit lawyer, call your state bar association and ask for its pro bono or charity committee. Or go online to their Web site, **www.abanet.org**. You can also ask the bigger nonprofits for recommendations.

testing the nonprofit water

Consider partnering with other nonprofits

Here's an idea: Before you take the plunge and start your own nonprofit, think about partnering up with an established nonprofit. This is especially recommended if you are not sure how long-term a commitment you want to make to your nonprofit. So if you are not sure, consider joining up with an established nonprofit organization and asking that it be your **fiscal agent**, or money partner. In a sense, the established nonprofit acts as your tax-exempt broker. And because it is a nonprofit—with a 501(c)(3) tax-exempt certification—you can also use it as a sponsor when applying for grant money. (For more on grants, see Chapter 10.)

Usually, established nonprofits charge a fee to act as a fiscal agent. This fee covers the administrative costs of being your agent and is usually 3% to 10% of whatever funding you receive. As you progress, you may find that you need more from your nonprofit sponsor—for example, office space, equipment, or help from its administrative staff. That kind of relationship is called a **partial association**, and often the percentage of fees is higher.

Another option is to become a local chapter of a national charity that works toward furthering the same cause that you are interested in pursuing. If there's no local chapter in your area, you can offer to start one and use national backing to bring your own local projects to fruition.

Other Ways to Get Started

Before becoming a full-fledged nonprofit, you can also start out by charging for your charitable services. Here's how it works: You charge those who can afford to pay for the product or service an amount of money that is of equal value to what they are receiving in exchange. For example, if you are trying to help immigrant workers with their English, then you would charge those who could afford it an hourly fee. The stream of income you get from those who can pay is then used to cover the costs of providing the exact same services to those who cannot afford to pay. For example, if you are going to provide counseling for physically abused women, you can charge those who can afford to pay the fair-market value and perhaps a bit more. You can then let them know that every $25 is going to help provide services for women who cannot afford counseling.

You can also charge fees on a sliding-scale basis, based on income or some other legitimate criterion.

Also, you can ask a wealthy individual or group to sponsor your work for a limited period of time until you can raise enough money to be independent. Then you can consider whether to become a nonprofit or for-profit business.

a nonprofit timeline

Plan the work flow

Okay, you have thought it over, and you have talked with others who either have started a nonprofit or work as a board member on one. You have talked with your friends and found a treasure trove of potential volunteers. You may have even talked with a nonprofit lawyer. You are certain that incorporating as a non-profit business is the best way to serve your idea. You are good to go! Terrific. Just know that it won't happen overnight. Like any business endeavor, starting a nonprofit take times. On average, it takes 6 to 12 months to get a tax-exempt nonprofit up and running. Here is a breakdown of the process:

1. Meet with your volunteer group and decide exactly what type of work your organization will be doing and who will be in charge of the various functions. Put these goals in writing; they will form the basis of your organization's bylaws, or rules of agreement. Find volunteers to be on your first board of directors.

2. Prepare articles of incorporation. This is a list of key information you draw up about your nonprofit, such as the nature of its work and the names of the officers, plus specifics on how your nonprofit will operate.

3. File for incorporation with your state's secretary of state business office by submitting your articles of incorporation. You want to file the nonprofit corporate form (called nonstock), which states that the money the nonprofit makes will not be paid out to share-holders, since the nonprofit will not have shareholders. There is usually a filing fee.

4. Apply to the IRS for an Employer Identification Number, or EIN. You will need to have this number to set up a bank account for your nonprofit as well as when you file taxes. It usually takes 10 to 30 days to get a number.

5. Meet with your board of directors and plan out your first year of programs, activities, or services, complete with a projected budget. Determine who on your board will prepare and file future tax returns to the IRS.

6. If you want to receive tax-deductible contributions and not pay federal income tax, you must file the form for your federal 501(c)(3) nonprofit tax exemption with the IRS. The IRS reviews applications as they come in. If your nonprofit is a simple organization and the forms are complete, the process can take 2 to 3 months. If the application is in need of a deeper review, the process can take 10 to 12 months or longer.

7. If you plan on doing a lot of bulk mailings, file for your mailing permit at the post office where you want to send out and pay for your mailings. This can be done in a day.

8. Set up a corporate bank account at your local bank using your EIN number as identification.

9. Create a logo. This will help you get instant recognition when people see your mailings and signs.

10. Get printed stationery bearing your logo, your mailing address, and telephone number.

11. Create a Web page, which will help establish the credibility of your nonprofit. Note: Some high-tech firms will donate this service to nonprofits.

now what do I do?
Answers to common questions

When I was interviewing a possible sponsoring organization for a reading series, I was offered a job on their staff to run practically the same project I was planning. Is this a good idea?

It can be, if the organization is sound and has a good reputation, and if you like the job as they describe it. After all, they will then take over the fundraising and the administration and leave you to devote yourself to the job you hoped to accomplish in the first place—with fringe benefits. But get it all in writing as a job description in your contract. That way, if their personnel and priorities change, you won't suddenly find yourself switched to another project without your consent.

What if there are other nonprofits that do what I want to do?

While you can expect competition for fundraising money, nonprofits generally do not compete in whom they serve. The more nonprofits there are to help meet the needs of the public, the better. Some nonprofits, however, do compete. For example, colleges vie for students, and hospitals compete for patients. You'll have to decide if you can succeed while competing for funding.

I want to start a nonprofit because my donors want the tax-deduction benefit. But I want to remain in charge of the nonprofit because it is my idea and my baby. What do I do?

Once you incorporate your nonprofit, you are formalizing your nonprofit and turning it into a public entity. You can be chair or president of the board of directors, but that position has a term limit, usually no more than three years, and you generally should not be paid in that capacity. If you wish to serve longer and be paid, you can consider becoming the executive director, or ED. The advantage of being the ED is that you can earn a salary doing what you love and you can do what you love for as long as the board of directors wants you to serve. But the disadvantage is that the board is in charge, and it can choose to fire you if you don't fulfill your work requirements. It is a tough choice, but one that you should consider prior to the incorporating process. Also, as an ED, you do not have the right to vote at board meetings. (If you decide to become the ED you should prepare a written employment contract.)

Can I draw a salary if I start a nonprofit?

Yes, you can. Just know that you will have to pay income tax on that salary, just as you would if you had started a for-profit business. However, nonprofits are started for the public good; you cannot start one to benefit or support an individual or family members. Also, the start-up years for a nonprofit are usually quite lean. Half of the nonprofits in the United States do not have a paid staff.

I want to start a nonprofit. What happens if I actually make money?

While profits are not the primary goal of a nonprofit, excess revenue does happily occur from time to time, usually due to an increase in donations by a fundraising activity. In the nonprofit world, this is referred to as a surplus, or an increase in the fund balance, and is plowed back into the nonprofit business and spent the next year.

Now where do I go?

CONTACTS

www.communitychange.org

www.irs.gov
or call their 501(c) division at 877-829-5500

www.idealist.org
The idealist.org is a great site "where the nonprofit worlds meet." Use it to find resources on everything from hiring consultants to managing volunteers.

BOOKS

Starting and Running a Nonprofit Organization
By Joan M. Hummel

Nonprofit Kit for Dummies
By Stan Hutton and Frances Phillips

2
Your mission

what's your mission?

Identify the problem

Chances are you have been working as a volunteer in a charitable nonprofit. And if you are like most nonprofit starters, you saw a need that was going unmet. Perhaps you have even started a few specific volunteer projects to help meet that need. But now you want to do something that will be ongoing to help that need. Great! What do you do next? The answer is simple: Start your own nonprofit business.

The first step is identifying the need. Be as specific as you can. The more you winnow the need down, the closer you will be to finding the core of your mission. For instance, say the local factory in your hometown shut down without warning and caused a huge rise in unemployment. People thrown out of work need help with job counseling, applying for federal aid, getting low-cost food, paying their bills, and more. You have an idea to help them get back on their feet by providing low-paying jobs.

There are nonprofit organizations out there you can turn to for guidance. Some are designed to meet complex social needs, such as shelter for the homeless or food for the hungry. But that doesn't mean you can't join in and provide your own specific nonprofit help. The most stable nonprofits offer services (have a mission) where there is an otherwise unfulfilled need.

Coming Up with a Goal

1. What exactly is the need or problem

2. Who would be served by meeting this need?

3. What do they have to say about the need?

4. How long has this need gone unmet?

5. What other volunteering is going on in light of this need?

6. Is there a nonprofit organization at work on this problem?

7. What has been done in the past to help with this problem?

8. Would this need be solved mostly by money, goods, or services?

9. What are the consequences of not meeting this need?

10. What obstacles might prevent you from fixing this problem?

11. Who could give you advice and help in solving this problem?

12. How much time do you want to spend fixing this need?

13. Is your family committed to helping you while you help others?

Note: Once you define your overall goal, it will form the basis of your mission statement (see page 34).

group involvement

Getting others on board

Starting a nonprofit can't be done in a vacuum. First, start talking with people who support you, think well of you, and of whom you think highly. They might be work colleagues or your running partners or your family members. Get people you trust to be your sounding board. This is not a time to impress anyone with your vision and ideas. And it isn't a time to shop for a mentor. The people you want to begin with are those who will listen to you seriously and will be thoughtful in their response to you. Ask them where they see strengths and weaknesses in your ideas. Ask them if they think this is a serious issue that needs to be addressed. Then ask if they know people who might be interested in getting in on the ground floor of your new organization.

Start close to home. Gather two to five people together in the same room at the same time to introduce them to one another. Talk to them about how they know you and about why they have a personal interest in solving the problem you are trying to address. As their trust grows, they will help you find any flaws in your thinking. Their collective wisdom will go into creating your vision and mission statements.

Note: This group of advisers will most likely become your first board of directors. This initial board of directors will be called upon to sign your articles of incorporation and to help you create the bylaws under which your nonprofit will run.

Future Board of Director Roles

The people you have gathered to help you work out the details of your nonprofit will ideally stay with you as you go forward. As you begin your organization and incorporate it (which is required to achieve tax-exempt status), there are four key roles you will need to fill:

President or Chair

Job: To provide leadership and direction to the board; ensures that all other board members understand and exercise their responsibilities.

Vice President or Vice Chair

Job: To ensure continuity in the leadership of the organization by supporting and assisting the president.

Treasurer

Job: To provide financial management and work out overall budgets for the nonprofit. To file tax forms with the IRS.

Secretary

Job: To keep ongoing records of board meetings. Also to handle correspondence of the membership and the board.

choosing your nonprofit's name

Your name can sell your mission

Most people who start a nonprofit organization have an idea for a name early on. But if you don't, that's okay. It will usually percolate up as you work on your goals. Ideally, the name should be easily identifiable with your new program and descriptive of what you do (or will be doing). Short and punchy also really helps! For example, The Society to Preserve and Encourage Radio Drama, Variety and Comedy very clearly states what it does in its title. But answering the telephone with this name would be awkward. So they use SPERDVAC as their acronym. The acronym might be easier to say when answering the telephone, but it immediately diminishes the clarity of what they do and who they are. So now what? You need to find a name that says it all and is short and sweet. For example, *Save the Whales, Husbands Against Domestic Violence,* or *Mothers Against Drunk Driving.* Think of a name that states what you do and/or where you'll do it or whom you will serve.

When you come up with several names you like, it is essential that you do a **name search** to make sure there are no other for-profits or nonprofits using the name you like best. Start checking by going online and typing in your proposed name into a search engine such as **Yahoo.com** or **Google.com**. If your name is not being used, then contact your state's secretary of state's office to check if there are any businesses using that name.

If you have your name, consider adding a tag line to it that describes the essence of your purpose. For example, Howard County Home Health and Hospice—
providing skilled and compassionate care in your home.

Your Web Name and Address

As you consider options for your organization's name, you'll also want to consider whether this name is available as a Web site address. This means searching your organization name possibilities as domain names. A domain name is an address on the Internet. As you are playing around with names, it is worth making sure yours isn't already taken. As you are choosing your organization name, make sure your preferred World Wide Web address is also available. This is why it helps to have at least two good options from which to choose.

If you Google "domain names," you'll get back more than 18 million sites that can help you determine if someone else already has registered your desired domain/organization name. Where do you register? There are dozens of sites accredited by the Internet governing body and hundreds of companies that resell the services under their own brand names. This makes the choice confusing unless you go to a good buyer's site. Here are two that make independent comparisons of domain registrars: RegSelect (**www.regselect.com**) and Domain Buyers Guide (**www.domainbuyersguide.com**).

When you register your domain name, you will be asked to pay a fee for one year. You can also buy in advance for 10 years just to make sure that no one else takes your domain name.

And remember, you want to register as a .org, not as a .com. The .org indicates that your organization is a nonprofit.

your vision statement

Honing your ideals

A vision statement is even broader than a mission statement. Imagine that you are in a spaceship flying high over the earth, looking back on the planet. Imagine you can see your town or city and the people you want to help or the problem you want to solve. The vision statement refers to the broad problem or issue: poverty, hunger, deforestation of the rain forest, lonely people aging without help. The vision statement defines the large boundaries within which your organization will work.

For example, a vision statement might be "Half of the population of Our Town lives at or below the poverty level. And it is estimated that within the next 25 years, an additional 15% of the population will fall below the poverty level." Then the mission statement might read: The Mission of the XYZ Organization is to provide three services to those who live at or below the poverty level in Our Town:

- Education about the services available to them

- Free transportation

- An emergency fund specifically for fuel/heat

The vision statement articulates the parameters or boundaries within which the organization is forming to operate. The mission statement then reflects the small part that this organization will play in addressing problems within these parameters.

Once the vision statement has been written to address the life crisis the organization is facing, and once the mission statement answers why your organization exists, then you can make an annual operations plan, a budget, a fundraising plan, a communications/marketing plan, and your calendar of what will happen when.

FIRST PERSON DISASTER STORY

Getting Help

We hired a consultant to help us raise money because our board was one of those saying that they give their time and so felt that they didn't need to give their money.

When she came in to meet with us, she asked us what our mission statement was, and could everyone please write it down. She had us compare them, and they were pretty close to what our real mission statement is.

Then she asked what our vision was. And that was the most astounding conversation—it actually got people hot! I was so shocked.

One board member said it was to erase illiteracy in our county. I guess I had thought that was our big vision, too. Well, the board member next to her jumped up and looked at her and said, "It is not! That's ridiculous! We can never erase all illiteracy. If we can keep the number of people who are illiterate to 10% or less, we'd be doing great!"

Well, the two of them had sat next to each other at monthly board meetings for years, and they had never been asked this question. It really shook everyone up that there was such a difference of opinion and that it wasn't something that could be brushed over; we had to deal with the two different views and consider other ones, too.

—Hannah P., Miami, FL

your mission statement

Defining what you are about

Having a mission statement is crucial to the long-term success of your organization. That's because a mission statement succinctly states what you do, where you do it, for whom you do it, and the special or unique ways in which you will do it.

Why is this so important? As you sit around the table creating your organization, everyone will be on the same page. But years from now, when the founder is no longer involved and the initial volunteers are no longer active, you will still want the essence for which your organization was created to be retained. A mission statement is the core organizing premise that is the glue for what your organization is and will be.

Part of the work in creating a mission statement will include discussions about what your organization is not, what services you will not provide or populations you won't serve. This is just as important a part of the discussion as what you will be, because in the discussion you may find that your original ideas can be improved by talking them through and out. You might be overlooking a group of people who need your organization or a group that will be negatively effecting when your organization is successful.

Another thing a mission statement needs to be is positively worded. It states what you will do, not what you don't do. Your planning documents or your board minutes can reflect what you won't be doing, but your mission statement is always positive.

A mission statement is also not an operations plan with a timetable. It does not state when the organization will end or what problems will be solved by when. It is broader than that. Although the mission statement might include geographic limitations, it does not need to. Usually geography is the only limiting description in a mission statement.

ASK THE EXPERTS

My group is arguing a lot over our mission statement. I am worried that they will offend someone.

The place to have disagreement is upfront and in the beginning, and just "among the family." The more you can draw out people's energy during this process the better. Reaching a consensus can be difficult, but it is vital if you want to keep your nonprofit on track. As you go out and seek new opinions or ask friends to volunteer or to give their money, you want most—if not all—of the disagreements settled so there is a united front and shared purpose.

How often can I change our mission statement?

Your mission statement should not change very frequently over the lifetime of your organization. Why? Because the mission statement is broad and encompassing, and although the operations may change from time to time or generation to generation, depending on your purpose, the overall mission of the organization should remain stable. Your mission statement should be reviewed and reaffirmed every two to three years and changed no more than three or four times in a 100-year period.

Does the mission statement become part of what is included when you officially incorporate?

Yes. Your mission statement or statement of purpose is included when incorporating and when filing for your tax-exempt status. It is essential that your mission statement have a charitable, religious, educational, and/or scientific purpose stated in it or the IRS will not grant you tax-exempt status.

writing your mission statement

Make it clear and concise

So how do you begin? Just like a journalist answering the who, what, where, when, why, and how questions. Start with your own experience and your own personal "testimony" about what has moved you to start an organization. How has this problem manifested itself in your life? Why do you care about the problem? What have you observed, felt, tasted, seen, smelled? What is pressing on you when you think about it or read about it or see it in action?

From there you will have two powerful tools that will ensure your organization's success: your first-person story that will move people to get involved and want to give their time, money, and support. And you will have a strong core statement about what you want the organization to accomplish. Once you are clear about what your new organization needs to address, you will also be clearer about what issues you might or might not want the organization to get involved in. This gray area will give you the opportunities to have great discussions with other people as you ask them to become involved with your new organization.

No mission statement is ever accomplished in one meeting unless only one person is attending the meeting! It usually takes three meetings and three to five weeks of thinking, writing, assimilating, discussing, and rewriting to reach a complete, compelling mission statement.

TIP: After each meeting, type up the common statements on one piece of paper. Pass these out at the beginning of the next meeting. This way the discussion will be more focused on the ideas rather than the personalities advocating for one side or the other. If, after a month of serious debate, consensus cannot be achieved, the founder can create the final mission statement.

Writing a Winning Mission Statement Step by Step

1. Gather your most interested friends, family, or future board members for a 3-4 hour meeting. Ask each one to take a few minutes to write down or to draw (if this is their communications style) their vision of what the nonprofit will look like when it is running at full capacity. Be sure to have them write their answers on large sheets of paper so you can put them up around the room.

2. Next ask them to describe the people being served and the place in which the services are being provided.

3. Next ask each of them to write what he or she thinks the organization should not do, whom it will not serve, the locations that will not be served.

When the writing is over, have each person describe his or her answers. Give each the same amount of time (5–7 minutes). As people talk, have someone note down the main points on a large piece of paper. Put checks or tally marks next to the main points that are repeated. You're probably onto something with these.

List the areas where there is disagreement and talk them through; the discussion is about the advantages and disadvantages of each approach, NOT about who is wrong or which opinion is right.

If there is conflict that cannot be resolved, ask one person to type up the common statements and e-mail or mail them to the group and ask everyone to think about the areas of disagreement.

Set your next meeting date—not for the next day, but let no more than two weeks elapse between meetings. Momentum counts.

At the second meeting, try to come to resolution. Work from the common statements and add the final elements as consensus is reached.

now what do I do?
Answers to common questions

I see mission statements everywhere now. Aren't they a bit silly?

Mission statements might seem silly when they are posted on a wall and no one pays attention to them. But it is the responsibility of the organization's leaders to make the mission statement valuable and relevant. If Coca-Cola and Habitat for Humanity and most churches have mission statements, there probably is some value in your organization having one, too.

How do we know if our mission statement makes sense?

Ask someone you trust (but who was not in the actual writing sessions) to review your mission statement. Then ask the following questions about the mission statement:

- Is it clear what the organization does and for whom?
- Does it state our uniqueness?
- Is it compelling?
- Will the mission statement stand the test of time?

I know some organizations have value statements. What are these?

Some organizations think it is important to describe the qualities with which services will be provided. For example, every client will be treated with respect; each species will be cared for as though it might be extinct within a decade; all patients will be served with tenderness, honesty, and in a confidential manner.

These values, or hallmarks, of service describe the tone in which the mission work will be carried out. They can be helpful by getting all the service workers on the same page, and they can be "enforced" by having every paid and unpaid staff member's job description state clearly how the values are to be realized and implemented through his or her work.

Now where do I go?

CONTACTS

The Internet Nonprofit Center
http://www.nonprofits.org/npofaq
The Internet Nonprofit Center has some ideas and articles about writing a mission statement.

Alliance for Nonprofit Management
http://www.allianceonline.org

The Association of Fundraising Professionals
http://www.afpnet.org

BOOKS

The Wilder Nonprofit Field Guide to Crafting Effective Mission and Vision Statements
By Emil Angelica

Mission Statements: A Guide to the Corporate and Nonprofit Sectors
By John W. Graham and Wendy C. Havlick

3

Your board of directors

your board

Your first board of directors

No nonprofit is an island. To work well, it needs group support from the very beginning. Enter your first board of directors, or founding board. Its job is to act as the trustee of your nonprofit. Specifically, the board's job is to:

- define the mission of your nonprofit (see page 34)

- draw up the **bylaws** or rules of operation (see page 52)

- brainstorm, oversee, and evaluate operations and programs

- set and approve the budget

- help with fundraising

- recruit other board members

Who makes up this board? Usually, a group of like-minded individuals who have a stake in the success of your nonprofit. For that reason, start with those closest to home: your family. In fact, most nonprofit founding boards have at least one relative of the founder on them. The next natural choice for board members is one or two of your closest friends.

As you move out from your circle of family and friends, you need to find people who are concerned about the problem your nonprofit is addressing. Where do you look? If your organization is wanting to help with young children's safety after school, then contact parents, teachers, and school officials of all the schools in your geographic area. Next look at the Web sites and annual reports of other nonprofits that do work similar to yours or that serve the same population but don't provide the same services. See if certain names start reappearing. It is from a list of these names that your founding board will come, as well as names you can ask to join the board in Year 2 or Year 3.

ASK THE EXPERTS

How many board members will I need?

In the beginning, start out small, say no fewer than 5, and then increase your board size as the nonprofit grows. (In most states, your bylaws can provide flexibility. For example, instead of specifying a set number, your bylaw could state that the board shall have no less than 5 and no more than 19. You can always vote to amend the bylaws to expand the size of the board when your organization matures. The average size of a nonprofit board is 17. Tip: The number should be odd, so there will not be vote ties that cannot be broken.

How often should my board of directors meet?

As often as needed to get the job done. In the beginning, your board will probably meet once a week. Once it is up and running, you can meet on a monthly basis. Finally, as your organization matures—in three to four years—your board should meet not less than every three months. Monthly is best, with additional committee meetings in between.

How long are meetings supposed to last?

Long, drawn-out board meetings can be the death knell of a nonprofit board. Keep your meetings to no more than two hours— one to one and a half hours is best. The best way to do that is to have a written agenda for each meeting. It's also a good idea to keep each meeting focused on one or two particular goals; for instance, naming the committees you will need and who will chair them can be the subject of one board meeting.

Where should we meet?

Most start-up nonprofits usually hold meetings in the founder's home. As your organization grows and you secure office space, you can meet there. Whatever you choose, you want to make sure it is a "neutral territory" and not conflict with any members' values.

best board qualities

Gathering winning people

If you are going to have a board of 11 people, how many of them need to be knowledgeable about and committed to what the organization does? Eleven.

How many need to be donors and resource gatherers? Eleven.

How many need to be numbers people, accountant types, financial planners? Not 11. Maybe 3 to 5.

How many need to be extroverts who like to speak publicly or writers who want to create the newsletter or the fundraising letter? Again not 11. Maybe 5 to 7.

How many need to be connected to a special group of people and willing to ask those people for help? Eleven, right?

If you go through the list of jobs to be done (look at your goals, objectives, and task lists) and begin to figure out how many people need what skills, you can put numbers by each type or skill set. Then you can recruit people who have passion about the cause and a special skill set the organization needs for the next one, two, or three years (a typical board term).

The number-one complaint board members have is that they do not know why they have been asked to be on that particular board. It frustrates them not to have a clear role or a clear assignment that they are expected to accomplish. When this level of frustration surfaces, board members will begin to miss meetings, with or without notice, and will fall away from active participation. Then it will be your job to help them resign while saving face. Avoid this common problem by being up front about what skills are needed on the board and by offering a place on the board to specific individuals who are willing to share those skills.

Five Qualities to Seek in a New Board Member

People may look good on paper, but how do you know if they'll make good board members? To identify stellar candidates, be sure they possess these five qualities:

1. Leadership orientation Leadership is hard to teach, so look for people who already have experience leading others (e.g., service on other boards or in other organizations).

2. Desire You need people who are willing to work hard, not rubber-stampers. Make that clear to prospects up front and be sure they want to invest the energy.

3. Skills in networking Board members can be your greatest resource. But that's only if they know how to network. Look for people willing to talk to their friends and colleagues about your nonprofit.

4. Ability to plan ahead Your organization won't survive long without planning for the future. It's essential that new board members know how to make long-term plans.

5. Business knowledge Many nonprofits operate like businesses these days. If new board members have concrete business knowledge (whether gained in the business or nonprofit sector), they'll be able to provide better guidance. —**Kathleen Leonard**

Kathleen Leonard is a regional trainer with Habitat for Humanity. Reprinted with permission from Nonprofit Board Report, *April 1997. Contact 800/220-5000.*

choosing officers

Your board members will help you make the initial organizing decisions. These are referred to as the bylaws, or terms of agreement. They include everything from how many members are needed to where the board is to meet and when. In these **bylaws**, you and your board will spell out which officers the board must have and the terms of the jobs of each officer (typically two years). It will also set the terms of office for each board member and say when and how board vacancies will be filled.

Most nonprofit boards include:
- Chair (this job usually falls to the founder)
- Vice chair (who fills in for the chair in his or her absence)
- Secretary (keeps records of the meetings)
- Treasurer (responsible for money and accounts)
- Board members (responsible for a myriad of volunteer duties)

Ideally, those board members who wish to be officers have skills that go with the job. For instance, in a perfect world, the treasurer knows about accounting and the secretary is a whiz at computers. But since board members are usually volunteers, you need to bear in mind that you may have to work with what you have. As your organization grows, you may need to hire staff to help you better fulfill your mission. While your board will not need to sign off on the hiring of support staff, such as administrators and accountants, it will need to hire the **executive director,** or ED, who will be responsible for the day-to-day operations of a nonprofit.

"Give, Get, or Get Off the Board"

This old adage says it all. While board members are not legally responsible for giving their own money, a nonprofit that does not have 100% financial participation by its board members puts itself in a weak position when going out and asking others to give money—assuming fundraising is an important goal. Foundations that give grant money will ask not only what percentage of board members give but how much the total board donates annually. And if your organization cannot state 100% participation, it is at a disadvantage to other organizations that have a financially committed board.

This is one of the most common problems nonprofit organizations face and is one that should be addressed up front and aboveboard. "We give our time and advice, don't ask for our money, too" is a typical answer many board members give when asked to give money. Founding board members will be giving time, advice, *and money* and asking their friends and family for money. By Year 3, board members will be giving their time, advice, money, and asking their friends and family for money. And by Year 30, the board will still be doing the same thing. This is part of the joy and importance of being a member of a board of directors. You are working to keep this organization alive. You are responsible for all levels of its success, including financial. This is an important job and not to be undertaken lightly or partially.

about committees

Dividing the task
makes it easier
to accomplish

As your board gets going, one of its first jobs (after naming officers) is to establish committees. Committees are the backbone of most nonprofits. Why? Because they are the ones that carry out key specific tasks. While most start-ups don't give a lot of power to their committees, they do need to empower their executive committee. It is composed of the officers of the board and needs to have the authority to make urgent business decisions. This is determined when creating your bylaws.

Some board committees can have nonboard members on them except for the finance committee, which shouldn't. So if the committees are too small to make recommendations to the board, people with specific skills can be asked to join a committee in order to perform specific tasks. This can be a great way to test future board members, because you will have experience working with them on a project or a committee and will know if they do what they say they are going to do and show up promptly for meetings.

Key Committees

Ideally, you want to match the skills of your board members with the jobs you need done in the following committees:

- **Executive committee:** includes all officers of the board.

- **Finance committee:** oversees the budget and keeps track of expenditures. Reviews the annual budget and may propose budgets.

- **Program committee:** works on creating new programs (services and good works) that will help further the nonprofit's mission and evaluates how well the current programs are doing.

- **Nominating committee:** identifies and mentors people to serve as board members.

- **Community relations committee:** keeps tabs on how the public views the nonprofit.

- **Fundraising committee:** plans ways to raise money for various key programs.

- **Volunteer committee:** recruits volunteers from the community for specific projects.

- **Marketing/promotions committee:** gets the word out. This might mean starting a newsletter, placing ads, and giving speeches.

- **Personnel committee:** reviews human resources needs, advises on salaries and benefits, writes policy and procedures for paid and volunteer staff.

your first meetings

Welcome, welcome, welcome

Today is the day your board of directors meets for the first time! Congratulations! You've done it! Your dream of a nonprofit is about to happen. So what should you plan for that first meeting?

For starters, if the meeting is at your house, set up a room with enough chairs. Provide simple refreshments, such as coffee and fruit. Next have paper and pens on hand. This meeting is about establishing the bylaws of your nonprofit. Here you will hammer out who, what, where, and when.

Start with Who: List people's names on name tags and introduce them to the others as they come in.

Next draw up a working agenda of what your founding board will need to cover in the next few meetings. If you can, get an easel board so that everyone can see the agenda; for example, Item 1: electing officers and selection of committee heads, Item 2: When, where, and length of next three meetings.

ASK THE EXPERTS

One of our prospective board members said she wouldn't participate if there wasn't insurance for board members. What is she talking about?

Most for-profit businesses have business liability insurance. This protects the business owners from all sorts of potential problems; for example, a lawsuit from a customer. The same need applies to nonprofits. Depending on the nature of your nonprofit and the laws of your state, your board members may or may not be liable for any suits incurred by the nonprofit. Because nonprofits are run by a board of directors, the people on your board can be named in lawsuits against the nonprofit. To spare your directors and officers from being personally sued, nonprofits can buy liability insurance for its board members. This insurance, called **directors and officers liability insurance** (or D and O insurance), protects individual board members. As your nonprofit grows, you need to discuss this issue with your board members.

Where can we go to find out about D and O insurance?

Call your local insurance agent and see if he or she can give you information about the costs and policies. Also, speak to your nonprofit attorney to determine if your organization requires it.

your bylaws

Your rules of how you run your nonprofit

The bylaws of any organization lay out in detail how the organization operates. The more you can decide up front about how you want your nonprofit to run, the better. Bylaws may seem overbearing, but they help enormously once you are up and running, because they state from the start how everyone agrees things should go.

Typical bylaws contain:

- The name of the organization

- The purpose of the organization (your mission)

- Where the offices are located

- Whether there are members and if so, what rights members have and how "member" will be defined

- When the annual meeting will be held and the rights of those who have a vote

- The powers of the board of directors

- Who can be a board member and their rights, term of office, nomination process, how vacancies will be filled, what defines a quorum, and rules about compensation and conflict of interest

- The terms, powers, vacancies, and responsibilities of each officer on your board

- Provisions for insurance indemnification of board members (see page 51)

- When the fiscal year begins and ends

- How the bylaws can be amended

- The dissolution and distribution of assets should the organization merge or end

Help with bylaws

The bylaws of your nonprofit are very similar to your articles of incorporation (see page 20). But you don't have to create these documents from scratch. Your state secretary of state's office or local community foundation will have copies of what needs to be included in both and probably some sample bylaws. Or ask three other nonprofits in your town for theirs. Then compare and contrast them. Want more help? It might be a good investment to hire a lawyer who is familiar with nonprofits to help walk you through this process.

Articles of Incorporation

Article I: Name of organization.

Article II: Mission.

Article III: Purposes.

Article IV: Membership. Define member, then list the different types of members you may have (e.g., active members, retired, student, affiliate). Also, state length of membership service, usually one year. List dues if any and a grace period for paying the dues.

Article V: Meetings of the membership. State how often the members shall meet, how many members may call a meeting, and how notice of meetings shall be given. Also state what makes up a quorum (typically 33% of membership).

Article VI: Committees. List names of committees and their composition. Typically, executive committee, membership committee, program committee, nominating committee, and public relations committee.

Article VII: Board of directors. Define powers and duties, eligibility, how vacancies will be filled, how officers will be removed from service (for example, a two-thirds vote of the board of directors), terms of office, and quorum number.

Article VIII: Officers and duties. Here you state the number of officers, then list each officer's duties separately.

Article IX: Code of ethical principles. Some nonprofits state their ethical codes, such as "foster cultural diversity and pluralist values," or "disclose all relationships which might constitute or appear to constitute conflicts of interest."

Article X: Amendments. State the process of how the bylaws shall be amended; for example, by a two-week notice to the board of the changes, followed by a two-thirds vote of the board.

Article XI: Dissolution of assets. How the nonprofit assets will be turned over; for example, remaining money will go to similar nonprofits.

Article XII: Limitations on activities. How nonprofit will use and not use its funds; e.g., no net earnings will benefit board members.

an advisory group

**Another source
of support**

Not all people will be ready or able to help. While their spirit is willing, their schedule is overbooked and they just don't have the time to be a board member. However, some of these folks would be glad to lend their name but do not want to have to attend monthly meetings and contribute time or money. Then there are some who will be desperate to be on your board, but you might be hesitant to put them on for any number of reasons.

Don't lose these lovely people. Instead, ask if you can add them to your informal advisory group. Advisors do only two things: They attend one fun, educational, and social event a year (like your annual meeting or your signature gala) where they are recognized for their contributions to your organization, and they are on call for you when you need them, their advice, their ideas, their connections, their address books, their introductions, or their ability to get media attention. Whatever special skill or gift they have, you want to have access to it as you need it or as they are willing to give it to you. Ask these folks to be a part of the advisory group or ambassadors for one year only. Then ask them again a year later if you still need them.

Who aren't they? Since an advisory group is not asked to do too much, they are not responsible for accomplishing a number of tasks on a deadline. They are not fiscally responsible for the health and stability of the organization. And they don't have to attend a lot of meetings.

Who are they? They are well-respected, gifted people who want to play a limited, targeted role for the organization.

FIRST PERSON SUCCESS STORY

Long on spirit, short on time

I have always been a huge fan of our local library. Members of the board do so many great things in our town. Last year they started a huge capital fundraising campaign. Since I was such an advocate, they asked me to serve on the fundraising committee. While I was honored to be asked, I knew I didn't have the time to serve properly. I work full-time, have a family, and have recently started to take care of my disabled brother.

I felt terrible about turning the library down. When I told the head of the board of my inability to serve, she said that she appreciated my honesty and that there was nothing worse than a volunteer who can't volunteer. She then suggested that given my time constraints, I become an ambassador to the library. This volunteer job is on a as-needed basis and reports only to her, the head of the board. There are no meetings to attend. My tasks would be to help her with various requests that I could manage, such as reviewing a grant proposal or helping organize a thank-you lunch for a retiring librarian, all on my schedule. I have been an ambassador now for five years. I love the work—it is interesting and varied. Best of all, I can help, without committing to a schedule. It's the best of both worlds.   **Dale S., Portsmouth, VA**

now what do I do?
Answers to common questions

I have got my board together, and we have written our mission statement and our bylaws. How do we keep our meetings on target?

Every meeting should start with an agenda. What do you want to accomplish? If you can't cover it in one hour, then you are not accomplishing objectives and tasks between meetings and are depending on the board meetings to do work. What happens at the meetings is the decision making that has to be made by the entire board gathered face-to-face.

Welcome by the board chair/president.

Approval of the minutes of the previous meeting.

Review of action tasks Each person states what they were to have accomplished by what date and whether they achieved their objectives or not.

Review of and approval of the budget (proposed and actual to date and compared to same time last year). Make sure the budget is in a type size that is easily readable.

Committee questions What decisions need to be made in this meeting in order to further the health of the organization? Committee reports can be sent in advance of the meetings. Do not read them aloud. Have the committee chair summarize them in five minutes or less.

Old business What business was left over from a previous meeting that can now be finalized?

New business What is coming up in the near future for the organization that needs to be presented at this meeting and approved or voted on at the next meeting?

Setting of next meeting date.

Close and thank you.

What if we don't have a quorum?

First of all, the board secretary needs to know what number makes up the quorum, or the minimum number of voting board members needed to have a meeting. This number should be laid out in your bylaws. A number of states have a legal statutory minimum number of people required to make a nonprofit quorum. Check with your secretary of state's office to determine if your state has a legal requirement. Most states require 33% of the total number of all current board members to be present for a viable meeting. So for example, if you can have a maximum of 21 board positions but only have 18 actual directors, you would have to have at least 6 voting members to do business at that meeting (33% of 18 is 6). What if you don't? You can still meet, but you cannot officially approve any action.

As the founder, I had a key task I wanted someone on my board to take over. When I raised it in the meeting, no one volunteered. What should I do?

Here's the rule: Board members make decisions as a group, but they participate as individuals. If you want a specific job done, then you need to go privately to a board member and ask. That is the only way to be sure that a leader will "step forward" to undertake the task. Then at the board meeting you can thank that member for stepping up to the leadership of that task.

Now where do I go?

CONTACTS

Idealist.org
The idealist.org is a great site "where the nonprofit worlds meet." Use it to find resources on everything from hiring consultants to managing volunteers.

Npgoodpractice.org
The Nonprofit Good Practice Guide web site provides information on managing a nonprofit.

www.boardsource.org
For information about building effective nonprofit boards.

BOOKS

The Nonprofit Leadership Team
By Fisher Howe

Starting and Running a Nonprofit Organization
By Joan M. Hummel

Managing the Non-Profit Organization: Principles and Practices
By Peter F. Drucker

4

Planning and financing

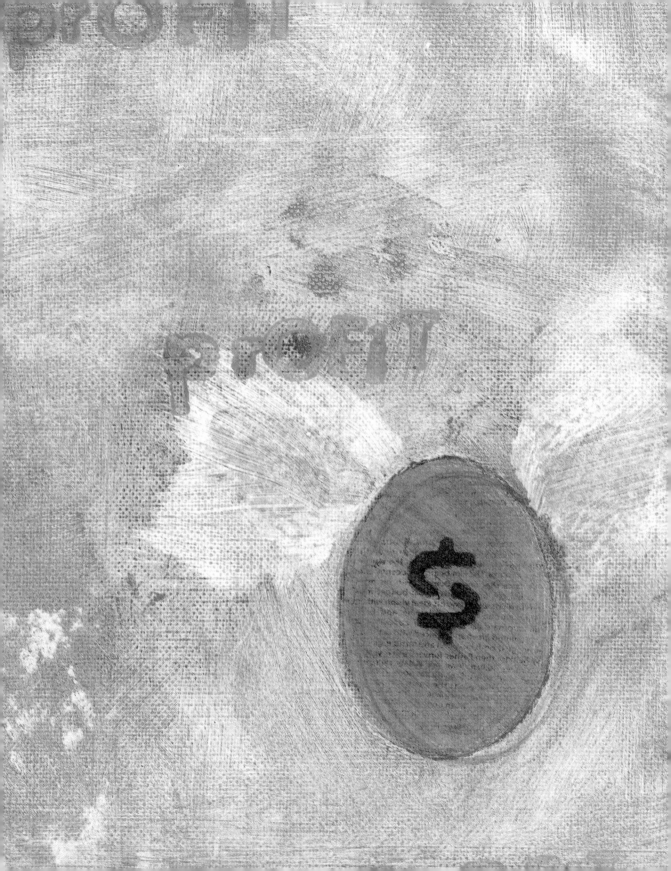

program planning

Your board of directors is in place, and you have worked very hard to create a working mission statement. From that mission statement will flow your **programs**—the actual work your nonprofit will be doing. You want to stay on target and not offer programs that don't reflect your mission.

So what mission-specific goals does your nonprofit hope to accomplish this year? The answer to that question will be your program's **objectives** for the year. If your mission statement is very specific (protecting county cats and dogs from abuse), you may have only one objective, such as rescuing elderly dogs who have been abandoned by their owners. If your mission is more broad-based, such as enriching the lives of disadvantaged children, your objectives will be more varied.

Meet with your board and brainstorm the top three objectives you want to achieve in a year. Keep your plans on the small side and accomplish your goals well and thoroughly. Then do bigger and larger. Nothing demoralizes volunteers and donors faster than an organization that tries to conquer the world and falls on its face because it tried to do too much too fast. Overcoming this type of failure is as difficult as overcoming the inertia of getting off the couch to start the January 1st exercise program. Set smaller goals and accomplish them first, then move on to the next level of goals.

Break It Down

Break your three objectives into doable **actions** with an agreed-upon **timetable** and **designated worker**. In other words, split the objectives into actual to-do actions, list them in order of the time needed to accomplish them, and then assign people who will be responsible.

Objective one: find homes for abandoned cats and dogs in the neighborhood.

1. **Action: Scout** the local ASPCA every week for abandoned dogs.
   Time frame: weekly.
   Designated worker: Mary G.

2. **Action: Draw up** a phone contact list of vets who will help provide medical care. Who will do it pro bono? Who will help with a sliding fee scale?
   Time frame: by end of the month.
   Designated worker: Mike F.

3. **Action: Research** animal rescue Web sites that you may partner with to help place your found animals.
   Time frame: End of quarter.
   Designated worker: Sarah C.

This detailed list of actions will form the basis of your nonprofit's calendar of events. Depending on the nature of your program, your calendar may call for the same tasks to be completed every week, or it may be seasonal—donating new books to disadvantaged children at holiday time is going to require a lot of work in the fall and winter months but will end in January. At the next board meeting, each volunteer (e.g. Mary G., Mike F., and Sarah C.) get to report on what each one achieved.

planning your budget

**How to pay for
your programs**

You have planned out your programs and broken them down into actual objectives for the year. Great! Now you need to plan how to pay for them. Every nonprofit needs money to do its work—be it money to pay for stationery for a one-time all-volunteer event or money for a four-year college scholarship program or money for a paid staff to manage that scholarship fund.

You need money to do your good work. Enter your annual budget. A budget is your nonprofit's vision described in numbers instead of words. It is what you hope to accomplish financially in a certain set period of time. Most nonprofits have monthly budgets, annual budgets, and then budget projections for the next two to four years. (When and if you file for tax-exempt status, the IRS will want to see your budgets for the previous four years. For a new non-profit, the IRS will want to see your current year's budget and your proposed budgets for the next two years.)

What goes into your budget? The cost of all the things you need to have in place in order to accomplish your program. That includes people (paid staff as well as money to train volunteers), space and equipment (an office, phone, etc.), publicity materials (including mailings, etc.). Your budget also includes how much money you hope to raise or be given; for example, a grant from a foundation. All these items will fall into two specific categories: revenues and costs.

What Makes Up a Budget?

- **Revenues:** This is the money you take in. It comes in three types:
  Earned revenues: for example, money your nonprofit earns from ticket sales or fees for program services.
  Contributed actual revenues: such as income from grants and individual contributions.
  Contributed in-kind revenues: such as donated equipment, goods, and services.

- **Costs:** This is the money you spend to accomplish your tasks. It comes in two types:
  Fixed costs: nonfluctuating costs you have to pay to run your organization; for example, rent and salaries. These costs remain fixed regardless of the level of your nonprofit's activity.
  Variable costs: costs that change with your nonprofit's activity and service level or fluctuate from month to month; for example, printing, postage, travel, heat, electricity.

No margin, no mission

When you subtract costs from revenues, you will get either a deficit or a surplus. Don't forget to factor in surplus money for next year so you can continue into the next year. As the saying goes in nonprofits, "No margin, no mission," meaning without extra money, your nonprofit work cannot continue.

tracking donations

Keeping donors happy

As your nonprofit first starts out, your budget will most likely be small, your costs low, and your donations on the slim side. Even so, it is important to keep good and accurate financial records for the organization. According to donors, this is one of the most valued characteristics in the charities they choose to support. Keeping good records is essential and not necessarily complicated in the first few years. It is similar to your personal accounting. There are a number of electronic programs that now tie the accounting part of a nonprofits activity with the donor-related components.

So what information do you need to keep?

- Income amount by event or source and date received

- Copies of the checks you receive

- A copy of the receipt you give each donor for cash contributions

- The specified purpose (if any) of the donor's gift

- All correspondence with the gift donor

In-kind donations

Not all donations need to be monetary. A great many nonprofits exist on donated goods and services, such as donated space and equipment. These are called in-kind donations, and you need to keep track of them just as you would a check. A corporate in-kind gift of a new computer, for instance, would be noted on the books as a donation at the price of a new computer. A donated used computer would be recorded at its assessed fair-market value. The time of your volunteers is also considered an in-kind donation. It, too, must be tracked. Why all this concern over in-kind gifts? Because when you add in-kind donations to your revenues, it shows a truer picture of your nonprofit's worth. And in some cases, seeing hefty in-kind donations can make the difference between getting a grant or not. (For more on grants, see pages 130–131).

Quid Pro Quo Receipts

Nonprofits that have been given tax-exempt status under section 501 (c) (3) of the IRS code (see page 84) may receive donations that donors can then claim as tax deductions. For example, when a donor writes a check for $100, all of that $100 goes toward the donor's charitable deduction. Your nonprofit notes all relevant information about the check in its files.

But what about more complicated donations, where the donor is paying in part for goods or services provided to the donor by the charity, such as a ticket to a gala ball or a music recital? How does your nonprofit account for these donations, called **quid pro quo** contributions, so that donors can file the correct charitable tax deduction when they file their income taxes? Here's the general rule: A nonprofit organization must provide a written disclosure statement to donors of a quid pro quo contribution in excess of $75. For example, if a donor gives $150 and receives a concert ticket valued at $40, the donor has made a quid pro quo contribution of $110. A disclosure statement must be filed because the donor's quid pro quo contribution exceeds $75. The required written disclosure statement must provide the following:

1. Inform the donor that the amount of the contribution that is deductible for federal income tax purposes is limited to the excess of any money (and the value of any property other than money) contributed by the donor over the value of goods or services provided by the charity, and

2. Provide the donor with a good faith estimate of the value of the goods or services that the donor received.

Check with your state's charity regulation agency to determine if your state has specific requirements about disclosure statements. Typically, charities must furnish the statement in connection with either the solicitation or the receipt of the quid pro quo contribution.

bookkeeping and accounting

Growing your nonprofit

As your nonprofit grows, it is very important to establish a book-keeping system to record all the financial transactions of your nonprofit in a financial ledger. It is imperative that your board of director appoint someone or hire someone to act as your bookkeeper. Most nonprofits use single-entry bookkeeping, sometimes called checkbook accounting, where only one entry is made in the financial ledger for each financial transaction. This is also known as cash accounting. Donations are recorded when they are received, and expenses are recorded when paid.

As your nonprofit grows, you can switch to the more sophisticated way to account for your transactions: **accrual accounting**. Here donations are recorded when they are promised, and expenses are recorded when they are incurred (which is usually before they are actually paid out). Why do this? Because time moves very slowly in the nonprofit world. To get a more accurate picture of how your nonprofit is doing, you need to subtract that element of time and see what money is due to come in and due to go out.

If money and accounting are not your thing, don't fret. Ask your financially savvy board members to help you hire someone to do this job. Ideally, you want someone who has lots of experience, great references, and a passion for accuracy.

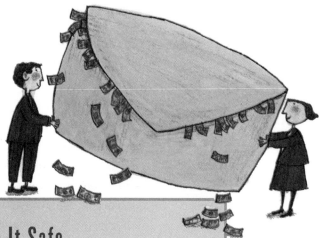

Keep It Smart, Keep It Safe

Here are a few simple things your nonprofit can do to ensure that cash and checks do not get misplaced or misrecorded.

Cash All cash transactions need to be recorded. Cash donations should be acknowledged by receipts—one to the donor and the other to be stored in a cash-receipt journal. These receipts should be numbered. It is also a good idea to file thank-you letters with these receipts. If you have a donor database, enter the receipt number and date into the database next to the donor's name.

Checks If your nonprofit receives a number of checks a month, you should get an endorsement stamp from your bank that says FOR DEPOSIT ONLY to the account of your nonprofit's name. When it comes to checks of a certain amount to be written by your nonprofit, be wise and get checks that require two signatures. Be cautious. The person who gets and/or opens the mail, logs it, and enters the information into the database should not be the only one who makes the bank deposit.

Note: You must create a system of checks and balances so no one can run off with an event's proceeds.

cash flow

It is important for the accountant or bookkeeper in the organization to have an idea of the cash-flow needs. Cash flow simply means the timing of when certain expenses will need to be paid and when certain pledges will be paid. So for example, the telephone bill, the utilities bill, and the rent can be scheduled. They come every month and are due within a certain time frame every month. The staff is paid on a regular basis: Weekly, biweekly, or monthly are the most common times. So you can project how much money you will need in order to pay for staff salaries.

What cannot always be predicted is what machine will break down or what car will need to be repaired or all the unanticipated yet common expenses. So it is helpful to keep at least three months' operating funds in the bank in case of emergency. This way, if an unexpected expenditure is required, you have enough money to cover the expense. Many organizations keep a savings account as well, to help with these expenses. Larger organizations have something called an endowment fund, the interest of which is used to pay for new programs or to pay for unexpected expenses.

Once you have determined when certain bills must be paid, you can project how much money you will need and when you will need it. The easiest way to keep money flowing in is through repeated mailings sent on a regular- and short-timed basis (like every month or every two months), and face-to-face solicitations with long-term donors who know what you do and the high quality of your work.

Net Assets

Accounting in the nonprofit world is similar to that of the for-profit world. There needs to be a tallying between your nonprofit's assets and liabilities. The difference between your assets and liabilities is called your **net assets**. You simply subtract assets from liabilities and the difference is called your net assets. There are three different types of net assets: **unrestricted** (money that can be spent as you or your board decide), **temporarily restricted** (money that can be used for a set purpose for a set period of time), and **permanently restricted** (money that can be used only for a designated purpose; for example, a grant for children's special education cannot be used to pay for your nonprofit's overhead).

types of budgets

Your nonprofit needs to have a budget. (The IRS will ask to see it anyway if you file for tax-exemption status.) There are two basic ways to format a budget.

1. Summary Budget
Based on your past history, you estimate how much you will take in and how much you will spend every three months. This type of budget is easy to do and is best for small nonprofits that offer only one or two services or programs.

Summary Budget Income	Summary Budget Expenses
Earned income	**Human resources**
Fees	Salaries
Contracts	FICA and benefits
	Temp workers
Contributed Income	**Facilities**
Individual donations	Rent
Foundation grants	Utilities
Corporate donations	
Government grants	**Other expenses**
	Postage
	Printing
	Travel
Total Estimated Income	**Total Estimated Expenses**

2. Program Budget

This budget is organized around each of the programs your non-profit offers. In other words, expenses are broken out for each and every program. This allows nonprofits to raise money separately for the programs it offers. It lets you divide the overall costs of annual operations by each program. So if Program 1 takes three staff people and 25% of the total office space, you can attribute 25% of the mortgage or rent to this program and all the salaries and support costs (like FICA) to this program. If Program 2 requires four people, then its program budget will need to reflect that, and the same goes for Program 3.

Program	Budgeted Percent of Total Budget	Budgeted Dollar Amount	Actual Dollars Spent	Actual Percent of Total Budget
Program 1	25%	$25,000	$24,457	23.5%
includes salaries, rent, insurance, and additional program expenses				
Program 2	30%	$30,000	$33,665	34%
includes salaries, rent, insurance, and additional program expenses				
Program 3	45%	$45,000	$47,828	48%
includes salaries, rent, insurance, and additional program expenses				
TOTAL	100%	$100,000	$105,950	105.5%

operating costs

Start-up nonprofits will usually have higher overhead than older nonprofits

Operating costs include everything from keeping the lights on to paying staff salaries and paying the mortgage or rent. With recent misappropriations by some well-known nonprofits, many self-appointed watchdogs are closely scrutinizing the overhead or administration figures of nonprofits. This is resulting in organizations stating that they spend no money on overhead or administration. This simply cannot be true. Every organization has fixed and variable costs associated with being in business: Telephones, postage, buildings and grounds maintenance, heating and cooling, and a variety of other boring, day-to-day expenses are necessary in order for staff to be accommodated and for services to be provided to clients. The goal is to keep the overhead costs as low as possible.

Salaries are almost always going to be the single most expensive item in any organization that needs people. Why? Because people are expensive and valuable. Add benefits such as health insurance or life insurance or pensions to the required payments for Social Security and FICA and you have anywhere from 50% to 90% of the annual operating budget of a typical nonprofit. The most effective nonprofits keep the ratio between operating costs and program costs at less than 15%.

Indirect Costs

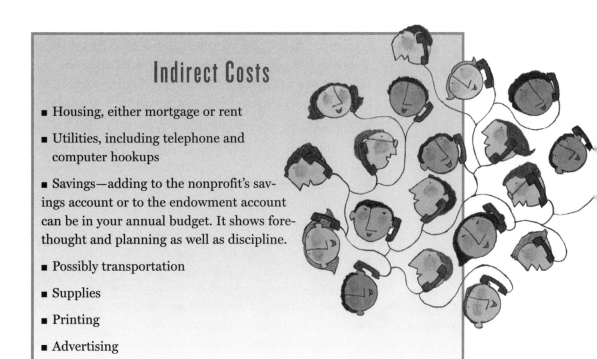

- Housing, either mortgage or rent

- Utilities, including telephone and computer hookups

- Savings—adding to the nonprofit's savings account or to the endowment account can be in your annual budget. It shows forethought and planning as well as discipline.

- Possibly transportation

- Supplies

- Printing

- Advertising

- Postage

- Other typical expenses that are not directly related to your mission or services

housing your nonprofit

Should the nonprofit buy a building or rent a space? Quite a few nonprofits like the idea of being fiscally responsible and owning their own building. And it has merit to build up equity in a structure that one day the organization could borrow against in order to buy a larger building or start another essential program.

Most nonprofits, however, do not want to be in the business of having to repair and maintain a building. It is easier to rent space and have someone else be responsible for the air-conditioning and heating units, the driveways and parking lots, snow removal, and all the additional responsibilities building ownership entails. Most organizations want to serve the people or mission they were created to serve and let others care for the building maintenance and repairs.

In the case of many colleges, universities, and hospitals that are nonprofits, they do own their own property. As nonprofits, these organizations are generally not required to pay property taxes. In the case of some huge campuses, this frustrates local politicians who want the tax base to improve by having these major employers and attractions pay taxes similar to those paid by homeowners or businesses. Many of these large nonprofits make a contribution to the town or city in which they reside in order to keep their relationship with the town healthy and happy, but this is not required.

Your best bet is to consider starting small and renting. Then as you grow, your board can create a long-term plan that may include buying or building a future home.

ASK THE EXPERTS

I want to start a nonprofit, and I have small children. Can I run the organization out of my home?

Yes, you can run it out of your home, and it might be possible for you to take a percent of your mortgage as a tax deduction or to receive "rent" from the nonprofit for the space you have given over to the organization. Many nonprofits start this way, but when you start going for big bucks, bear in mind that it won't look good to funders to see that you are receiving income or rent. Keep the boundaries clean and wide. As soon as you are able, move your nonprofit out of your home. A nonprofit needs visibility and a sense of ownership by its staff and volunteers. Moreover, your nonprofit space must be up to code for liability and disability reasons, and most private homes are not.

I have found a church that is willing to offer me free space for my new organization to help the homeless. How do I account for this space?

Many churches, synagogues, and similar organizations will try to make space available to organizations that do good work and don't violate their religious principles. To find out what the fair-market value of the space is in your town, ask five to eight other businesses how much they pay for rent and divide that number by how many square feet they have. Make an average of their rent by square feet and then apply it to your office space. Show this as an in-kind gift on your budget and in your annual report. (See page 128 for information on in-kind donations.) Send the church a thank-you note and tell its members how successful your organization has been. Don't forget to be a good neighbor and ask them about their building-use policies. For example, some don't allow use of their facilities after business hours. Also, be sure to get your own insurance policies against theft and fire.

being audited

When you want to
ensure everything is
shipshape

Most nonprofit start-ups as well as those whose revenues do not exceed $5,000 do not need a formal annual audit by a certified public accountant (CPA) who will spend time and money going over the accuracy and completeness of your nonprofit's financial information. Instead, those board members who are responsible for the nonprofit's books can review them and present their findings at a yearly budget meeting.

But as your nonprofit grows, you may find that donors and grant-makers will request to see annual audits in order to review your financial policies. In order to get a grant or a large donation, you may have to include a letter from a CPA who has reviewed your books and given your nonprofit the seal of approval.

What does a formal audit provide? An audit usually includes the following:

■ A cover letter, signed by the auditor, stating that your financial affairs are in order.

■ The financial statements, including the statement of financial position (balance sheet), statement of financial activity (income statement), and statement of cash flow. Health and social service organizations also have a statement of functional expenses. Many audits show comparative information between fiscal years.

■ Notes to the financial statements, which might include information about functional expenses, a depreciation schedule, further information about contributions, volunteer services, and other significant information not obvious in the financial statements.

In addition to the materials included in the audit report, the auditor often prepares what is called a management letter or report to the board of directors. This report cites areas in the organization's internal accounting control system that the auditor evaluates as being weak.

What an Auditor Does

The auditor will request information from individuals and institutions to confirm bank balances, contribution amounts, conditions and restrictions, contractual obligations, and monies owed to and by your organization. The auditor will review physical assets, journals and ledgers, and board minutes to ensure that all activity with significant financial implications is adequately disclosed in the financial statements. In addition, the auditor will select a sample of financial transactions to determine whether there is proper documentation and whether the transaction was posted correctly into the books. In addition, the auditor will interview key personnel and read the procedures manual, if one exists, to determine whether the organization's internal accounting control system is adequate. The auditor usually spends several days at the organization's office looking over records and checking for completeness.

Auditors are not expected to guarantee that 100% of the transactions are recorded correctly. They are required only to express an opinion as to whether the financial statements, taken as a whole, give a fair representation of the organization's financial picture. In addition, audits are not intended to discover embezzlements or other illegal acts. Therefore, a "clean" or unqualified opinion should not be interpreted as an assurance that such problems do not exist.

Many auditors provide nonprofits with year-end financial management services which are not part of the audit. These include preparing:

- year-end financial statements based on client records

- notes to the financial statements

- depreciation schedules

- accrual and other adjustments based on client information

Note: If your nonprofit would like an audit, be sure to interview at least three CPA firms with nonprofit experience.

now what do I do?
Answers to common questions

How do we account for donated professional services?

Usually, donated services are not "accounted" for. What this means is that services that a professional donates to your organization cannot be taken as a tax deduction by the professional donor. For example, a professional CPA cannot donate the time he spends doing your bookkeeping and claim that time as his gift to your organization on his taxes. If you wish to compensate him, you can determine the fair-market value of the time or service and then reward the donor with benefits, such as free tickets to your next gala, but this is strictly your board's decision. Note: It is illegal for the donor to send you a bill and have you pay the bill with the intention of his turning around and contributing that amount back to you. Please check with your lawyer and accountant for specific details on this issue.

My staff is balking at the idea of having to allocate their time between our four programs. How can I convince them that this is important?

There are two solutions to this problem. The first is to communicate with the staff regularly about the grants that the organization is receiving and how their time-keeping records contributed directly to this success. The second solution is to make it easy and fun. Give weekly rewards for those who turn in their tracking reports first or on time (it might be a free-lunch coupon or an hour's comp time) and set up a form that they find user-friendly. Then spend the time to translate it into a comprehensive report for the board, donors, and grantors. The burden is then shifted to you (or perhaps a volunteer can do this?), but you will get what you need.

We are hoping to get a really large grant from the government. In order to get it, we have to change our accounting system from summary to program. Do we have to do that?

Yes. Large grants—anything over $100,000—require that you show program cost allocations. You should also expect to be audited.

Now where do I go?

CONTACTS

Financial Accounting Standards Board
www.FASB.org

Their mission is to establish and improve standards of financial accounting and reporting for the guidance and education of the public, including issuers, auditors, and users of financial information. Nonprofits should keep their records as guided by the FASB. Your accountant can help you organize your records by FASB standards.

Governmental Accounting Standards Board
www.GASB.org

Their mission is to establish and improve standards of state and local governmental accounting and financial reporting that will result in useful information for users of financial reports and guide and educate the public, including issuers, auditors, and users of those financial reports.

BOOKS

Wiley Not-for-Profit GAAP 2004: Interpretation and Application of Generally Accepted Accounting Principles for Not-for-Profit Organizations
By Richard F. Larkin and Marie DiTommaso

Not-for-Profit Accounting Made Easy
By Warren Ruppel

The Budget-Building Book for Nonprofits: A Step-by-Step Guide for Managers and Boards (Jossey-Bass Nonprofit & Public Management Series)
By Murray Dropkin and Bill LaTouche

Guide to Audits of Nonprofit Organizations
By D. R. Carmichael et al.

Basic Financial Skills: Understanding and Presenting Financial Information
By Jennifer Bean and Lascelles Hussey

5
Incorporating and tax filing

federal
state
city

?

incorporating explained

Drawing up your articles of incorporation

Incorporating essentially makes your nonprofit a legal entity. It's the first step to making your nonprofit a reality. For the hassle of incorporating, you are offered some very valuable benefits. Incorporating limits the liabilities of those who run the nonprofit, it ensures that the nonprofit will continue until it is legally dissolved, and it's necessary if you wish to apply for tax-exempt status.

In order to incorporate, one person—you—(called the **incorporator**) writes up your **articles of incorporation** and mails them, along with a fee, to your secretary of state's office or other state office that handles business incorporations. (This office usually handles applications both for nonprofit and for-profit incorporations.) Once you are approved, you will apply for and be issued an employer identification number, or EIN, from the IRS, which is merely the numerical identification of your business for tax purposes. Among other things, you will need that EIN if you open a corporate bank account. (All businesses have an EIN; it has nothing to do with getting tax-exempt status. Think of it as a Social Security number for a business.)

What are these articles of incorporation? Nothing mysterious. If you have drawn up your bylaws, you have pretty much all the information that is in them. It is just a legal record of the name, address, and purpose of your business.

What should your articles of incorporation include? There are lots of examples to consider. Just ask to see the articles of an organization that is similar to yours. If you are still in doubt, have a nonprofit lawyer draw up your articles and/or check your application. (See page 17 for information about nonprofit lawyers.)

TIP: It is vital that you check your state's rules about incorporating nonprofits. Each state has its own rules and requirements about what is needed and how to proceed. For a link to your state's secretary of state, go to **www.nass.org/505/sosflags.html**.

Standard Articles of Incorporation

While your articles can vary, they usually all cover the same ground. Each item is marked by a roman numeral. Here is a sampling:

I. The corporate name of the organization.

II. The street address of operations and the mailing address if different and the registered agent. This is the person who will be served with a copy of any legal work regarding the corporation.

III. The name and address of each incorporator (usually a founding board member).

IV. Whether or not the corporation will have members (these are people who are not on the board of directors). Most nonprofits do not have members.

V. The broad purpose of the organization. For example, "To provide educational programs for the underprivileged in accordance with the IRS code."

VI. Who will be the registered agent for the nonprofit.

VII. How the articles will be amended.

VIII. What happens if the nonprofit dissolves. The IRS requires a statement that on dissolution of your nonprofit the assets will be transferred to another 501 (c) (3).

who gets an IRS exemption

The reasoning behind the tax benefit

Our government cannot afford to provide all the social welfare programs that the independent (nonprofit) sector can at such a reasonable cost. To encourage these charitable organizations and those donors who contribute to them, the IRS grants these organizations a special tax status. This status means that the organization does not have to pay federal "income taxes" on its goods or services provided to help others. It also generally does not have to pay state and local taxes on any property it owns. The biggest benefit, however, is that donors (be they individuals, corporations, foundations, or governments) will not give repeated significant contributions if your organization is not exempt.

The IRS grants a federal tax exemption to charitable, education, scientific, and other specific types of organizations because they work for the common good or the greater good. These nonprofits may be exempt under the IRS Tax Code Section 501 (c) (3). Other types of nonprofits are also recognized as exempt under different sections of the Internal Revenue Code, but each one has to apply for exemption.

Classifications for 501(c) Nonprofits

The IRS has different numerical classifications for 501 (c) nonprofits; which one depends on the constituency they serve. Here's a sample:

501 (c) (3)	serve charitable, religious, education, scientific, or literary organizations
501 (c) (4)	civic leagues and social welfare organizations
501 (c) (5)	labor, agricultural, and horticultural organizations
501 (c) (6)	business leagues
501 (c) (7)	social and recreation clubs
501 (c) (8 & 10)	fraternal beneficiary societies and domestic fraternal societies
501 (c) (11)	teachers' retirement fund associations
501 (c) (12)	local benevolent life insurance associations, mutual irrigation and telephone companies, and like organizations
501 (c) (13)	cemetery companies
501 (c) (14)	credit unions and other mutual financial organizations
501 (c) (19)	veterans' organizations
501 (c) (20)	group legal-services plan organizations
501 (c) (21)	black lung benefit trusts
501 (c) (25)	title-holding corporations for multiple parents
501 (c) (26)	state-sponsored high-risk health coverage organizations
501 (c) (27)	state-sponsored workers' compensation and reinsurance organizations

applying for tax exemption

Remember, it lets donors deduct their donations

For most start-ups, filing for tax exemption is a top priority. That's because having that tax status allows donors to give more freely, as they can then write off their donation on their taxes. Also, many non-profits operate on such a thin margin that not paying taxes can mean the difference between staying in business or folding.

What do you need to do? You need to fill out the IRS form 1023. This form was revised in 2004 and is more detailed than the old form because the IRS hopes to not have to contact you with any questions about your application. This will save time and money. You can download form 1023 at **www.irs.gov** or try **idealist.org**. There is a $500 filing fee; however, those nonprofits that plan to have less than $10,000 in gross receipts for each of their first four years will pay a fee of $150.

If your nonprofit is a 501 (c) (4) or a civic or social welfare organization, such as a volunteer firefighter department or a homeowner's association or a town beautification society, then it should file form 1024. Other associated nonprofits, such as veterans' associations, also need to file 1024.

Brace yourself. The 1023 and 1024 forms are long. The 1023 is nine pages long with a number of schedules. If this seems overwhelming, consider hiring a nonprofit lawyer to help you file (see page 17).

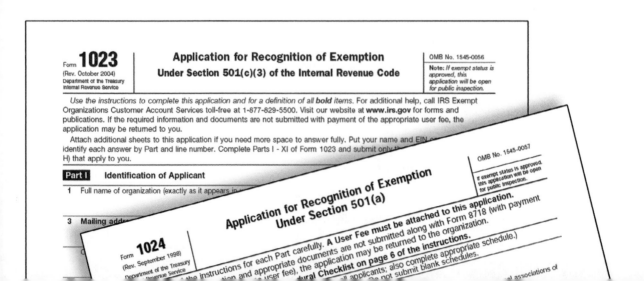

What's in Your Filing Package:

- A completed 1023 form

- A copy of your articles of incorporation (see pages 82–83)

- A copy of your bylaws (see page 52)

- Your EIN number

- A statement that shows you have an organizational conflict-of-interest policy so that it is clear that no one in your nonprofit is personally benefiting

- A projected two-year budget. (Take a deep breath. Drawing up a budget is not as hard as you might think; see page 62. If you have been open for three years already, then you need to submit your last three annual reports.)

- Copies of any leases or contracts or agreements your nonprofit has entered into

Specific details about your past, present, and planned activities

ASK THE EXPERTS

How long will it take to learn whether the IRS will grant our nonprofit tax exemption?

It takes on average four to six months for the IRS to respond to tax-exemption status filings. The rule of thumb is, the more complicated the organization and its finances, the longer it will take to get approvals. What causes problems is proving to the IRS that you have public support funding. To expedite matters, you can get an advance ruling letter from the IRS. This is usually granted to organizations that expect to get public support and that submit all the estimated budget projections showing future anticipated income from the public but have no track record. The IRS might grant this determination (for five years), and at the end of that time you must show that in fact you did receive public support. If you cannot show that, it means you will be considered a private charity and will be under the additional scrutiny of a private foundation. It, however, doesn't mean you aren't a 501 (c) organization. You still are, but you will be considered private, not public.

more exemptions

More benefits for your organizations

Every nonprofit that is granted an IRS tax exemption will be exempt from paying federal taxes. But that doesn't mean your non-profit will automatically be granted exemption from state income taxes or state sales taxes. Getting relief from those taxes is up to your state laws. It is not uncommon for nonprofits to be given relief from federal taxes and certain state taxes, but not state sales taxes.

You can also get a break on mailing. Nonprofits are allowed to use the bulk mail rate for first-class letters. Once you have your tax exemption, you simply go to your local post office and show your tax-exemption qualifying letter from the IRS.

One huge benefit of being tax-exempt is that it allows your non-profit to be eligible to receive tax-deductible contributions. This is a great incentive for many donors.

And another huge "benefit" to your organization is that as an established tax-exempt nonprofit organization, you will attract volunteers who will work hard to serve your clients. These volunteers will not expect to be paid for their work. This is unpaid work that they do out of their own desire to help. This is unique to charitable organizations and nonprofits.

ASK THE EXPERTS

Our nonprofit sells lunches at our educational programs. Just last week, we got a back tax bill for $5,000 for sales tax for those lunches. We don't have the money. What can we do?

It is very important to pay attention to exactly what you will need to pay taxes on. Many nonprofits make the mistake of assuming that because they are tax-exempt, they don't need to pay any taxes. When their state IRS office catches up to them, they often owe back taxes. If the bill is onerous, go to your state attorney's office or IRS and plead your case and ask for forgiveness of the tax bill. Failing that, work out a schedule of payments with the IRS and ask for relief from any penalties.

What if the IRS rejects our application?

The IRS is looking for red flags in your filing; for example, if your board members are going to receive salaries or if there is only one board member. If you clear those up, you can reapply with a new application. If that application is rejected, you can write a letter to the IRS outlining why you think its decision is wrong, based upon the law and your facts. If you still aren't satisfied, you can appeal the decision in United States Tax Court.

working out your projected budget

Go with expenses or go with revenues

Generally, the vast majority of the money contributed to your nonprofit in its first few months will go toward **programs** or the actual work (services or goods) provided by your nonprofit. How do you plan to account for getting and spending this money in your projected budgets? The IRS requires four years of actual or three years of projected budgets.

You have two choices. You can either start with your projected expenses and then figure out what your projected revenues will need to be. Or you can start with projected revenues and then draw up a list of expenses that you can afford, based on the money you are fairly certain you can raise.

One expense you will most likely need to factor in is insurance. Even though incorporating your nonprofit does shield you from certain liabilities, that shield applies only to the nonprofit's income or assets. In other words, the nonprofit can cover liabilities up to the extent of any income or assets it has, including property. Therefore, it's a prudent idea to consider buying insurance, such as business liability insurance, property insurance (if your nonprofit owns property), and directors and officers liability insurance. This insurance protects board members from personal liability. (For more on insurance, see page 51.)

Sample Projected Budget

Start by drawing up a list of items you are sure about. Check your list with other nonprofit budgets. (You can find those budgets by going online and tracking their IRS returns. Nonprofits are required to make their tax returns public.) Try to figure the amounts on a monthly basis. You may be surprised at how expenses will differ depending on the season.

Expenses First

Phone

Postage (estimate of weekly mailing)

Liability insurance (for more on this see page 51)

Advertising for fundraiser

Conferences

Travel

Fees (for IRS filing, annual memberships, etc.)

Salaries

Projected Revenues First

Fees from clients

Government contracts

Grant money

Contributed supplies or equipment (called in-kind donations)

Individual or donor contributions

Event contributions

the IRS test

Where is your money coming from?

There are now 1.8 million tax-exempt organizations in the United States, and that number is growing by the hundreds of thousands each year. How does the IRS determine who is a legitimate non-profit, deserving of tax exemptions? Depending on whom they serve and who gives them money, the IRS will first test and then classify each nonprofit business as it applies for tax-exempt status, and thereafter nonprofits must strive each year to maintain that hard-won tax-exempt status.

When and if you decide to apply for tax-exempt status, it is important to know that the IRS will ask you to check which type of non-profit you want to be; for example, a museum or an educational charity. Next it will look at your projected budget to determine how much of the money you will need to operate will come from the public. The IRS calls this the **public support test**. Passing this test will have a big impact on your finances and how much or how little money you will need to raise in order to stay a nonprofit. To pass the public support test, at least one-third of your donations must come from government agencies, or grants from public-supported agencies, or donations from the public; for example, people who walk in to tour your museum.

If you don't pass that test or prove that you are close to passing it with future fundraising programs, you may be classified as a "private foundation." Every nonprofit tax-exempt 501 (c) (3) is either a public charity or a private foundation. If the nonprofit otherwise qualifies for tax-exempt status (for example, for educational purposes), the public support test will not affect your exempt status.

FIRST PERSON INSIGHTS

The right person for the right job

It was our first year in business as a nonprofit. We were lucky to have several volunteers who had business skills we vitally needed. Well, all except one. We had a volunteer who offered to help us keep the records of our income and expenditures. She had been a bookkeeper for a small business in town for years, and our organization helped her out when she was in some difficulties. The problem was we really wanted to keep our records electronically, but she only liked to use an old-fashioned calculator, pencil, and paper. As the head of the board, I had to make a decision. I knew from filing for our tax-exempt status, how much easier it would to use the computer, so I knew we had to stay with the computer or jeopardize our operation. I also knew we had to find money to pay for a computer-savvy bookkeeper, hopefully at a reduced rate. I was overcome with guilt. How could I turn down her generous offer? Yes, the accounting of money and financial records has to be paramount in a nonprofit, but I so didn't want to hurt her feelings. I took the problem to the board. One member suggested that it would be a good idea to have two people for checks and balances. So I asked her if she could double-check the work done by our future bookkeeper. She agreed. In time, she learned a lot about using the computer, which has proved a boon to her job skills.

Mackenzie C., Sarasota, FL

your annual filing

Filing your first tax return

Great, you got your exemption. You are now a bona fide tax-exempt nonprofit. Good for you! Now what? Generally, tax-exempt organizations must file an annual return. At least it is not quarterly, as it is for for-profit businesses.

Since a nonprofit is not paying federal taxes, it needs to file what is called an **exempt information return**, otherwise known as the form 990. In fact, those public nonprofits that have $25,000 or more in gross receipts must file an exempt-organization information return. This return is due on the fifteenth day of the fifth month after the end of your organization's fiscal year.

At the end of your nonprofit's first year, your board (usually the treasurer) makes a financial and program report. This report contains information about who was served, how services were provided, how much was raised, and how much money was spent on expenses. The crux of this information will be used when filing your annual tax return.

The good news is that since 2004, when the IRS overhauled its nonprofit filing forms, the form 990 has been greatly simplified to make filing a whole lot easier. There is even a 990 EZ form for those nonprofits that make less than $100,000 in annual gross receipts.

Your state's secretary of state may also require your corporation to file an annual report. You may be able to check requirements online, and in many states you can even file your annual report online as well.

ASK THE EXPERTS

My job is to file the tax return for our nonprofit. I have never even seen one of these. Where do I get the form?

Go to **IRS.gov** and type in form 990. You will get a PDF of the form you can download and print out and then mail completed into the IRS. Or you an file electronically if you wish.

Can I get an extension on filing our annual tax return?

The due date may be extended for three months, without showing cause, by filing form 8868 before the due date; an additional three-month extension may be requested on form 8868 if the organization shows reasonable cause why the return cannot be filed by the extended due date.

Is there any way I can see how other nonprofits filled out their tax returns?

Tax returns for nonprofits are public documents. You can go online at **www.grantsmart.org** and find the returns of more than 50,000 public nonprofits and private foundations. This is a great way to learn how other nonprofits operate.

Are there any forms I need to file quarterly?

Yes. If your nonprofit has any unrelated nonprofit business income (UBIT), it must report that quarterly. Also, if you have paid employees, you will need to file quarterly withholding taxes. (For more on paid staff, see pages 188–189.)

now what do I do?

Answers to common questions

Do I get a tax-exempt number for my organization?

No. Unlike some states that issue numbers to organizations to indicate that these organizations are exempt from state sales taxes, the IRS does not issue numbers specifically for exempt organizations. Rather it sends a letter stating you are tax-exempt. You will need to show a copy of that letter when you prove your tax-exempt status; for example, when applying for a grant.

How can my application for tax-exempt status be expedited?

Requests for expedited treatment of an application must be made in writing and must contain a compelling reason why the case should be worked ahead of other applications. Generally, expedited treatment will be granted in the following circumstances:

■ A grant to the applicant is pending and the failure to secure the grant may have an adverse impact on the organization's ability to continue operations.

■ The purpose of the newly created organization is to provide disaster relief to victims of emergencies, such as flood and hurricane.

■ There have been undue delays in issuing a letter caused by problems within the IRS.

■ Any other situation where the IRS feels expedited service is warranted.

Should we use our mission statement for our "exempt purpose"?

The IRS form 1023 asks you to provide a document stating the purpose of your nonprofit. It requires that you supply this answer in something it calls "exempt purpose language." This is very explicit language that you need to use in order to pass its purpose test. The language in your mission statement will hopefully be a bit more inspiring than what is required for this purpose clause, so don't simply cut and paste in your mission statement. Check out the IRS Web site for help with writing the purpose clause.

Our nonprofit wants to start another nonprofit to serve a whole different group of clients. Do we need to file for a new EIN and tax exemption for this new nonprofit?

If your new project is going to dramatically diverge from your current mission statement that you gave to the IRS when you filed, then yes, start a new, separate organization with its own EIN and separate checking account. Act as though you are going to begin a new 501 (c) organization and file with the IRS for tax exemption.

If, however, the new program is tangential to what you are already doing or is simply a new population that you wish to help and the programming will remain the same, you do not need to get another EIN or start a new organization. It's a good idea, however, to expand your mission statement (reflect the changes in the minutes of the board meeting, along with who participated in the organization-wide discussions). And don't forget to change your logo or tag line to reflect this expansion of your original mission. The new change should be a reason to celebrate and go to the community and media with the exciting news of the growth of your organization as it responds to the needs of the community. (For more on Staging a Special Event, see pages 146–147.)

Now where do I go?

CONTACTS

Idealist.org
The idealist.org is a great site "where the nonprofit worlds meet." Use it to find resources on everything from hiring consultants to managing volunteers.

www.fdncenter.org
This is the Web site of The Foundation Center. It has lots of info on how to write grants and search for donors.

BOOKS

The Nonprofit Handbook
By Gary M. Grobman

Starting and Running a Nonprofit organization
By Joan M. Hummel

6

Working with volunteers

finding volunteers

Ask a volunteer to ask two friends

How do you "hire" volunteers? The best plan is to recruit volunteers from at least three of the groups that are benefiting from your nonprofit. For instance, if your nonprofit is providing after-school care for neighborhood children at your church, there are three natural groups to recruit as volunteers: the children's teachers, the children's parents and family members, and your fellow church members.

Once you know your core volunteer groups, you are on your way. How do you get volunteers on board? Here's a tried-and-true answer: Get one on board and then ask him to get a friend to join in the fun and work. There is nothing like a peer asking a peer to join in a volunteering task. Better still, have two volunteers ask a mutual friend. It is hard to turn down two friends at the same time.

You can also "advertise" for volunteers in public places like local newspapers and magazines or radio. Don't forget to leave flyers in local coffee shops and grocery stores asking for volunteers.

Be sure to share the recruitment of volunteers with your board members. Bringing in volunteers will give your board members more buy-in to the success of your nonprofit. Ideally, you want to have a surplus of volunteer names to contact as needed. Having the ability to find an extra pair of hands quickly can make all the difference in the life of a nonprofit. If a crisis happens, you can call for backup so your nonprofit won't have to temporarily slow or shut down.

Volunteers are vital to the success of most nonprofits. In fact, volunteer time will most likely be your largest indirect cost. (For more on this, see Chapter 4.) Keep good records of the hours volunteers work.

FIRST PERSON DISASTER STORY

Volunteering with heart

I have been a volunteer pretty much all my life. I volunteered as a child, throughout high school, and in college. It is a part of who I am and what my family taught me to be important. I've had many wonderful experiences helping people and being thanked and appreciated by the organizations I have worked for.

But the best experience I ever had was with a hospice organization. I was trained for two full days in the best practices and dos and don'ts of volunteering with the dying. I was a respite caregiver so I sat with a patient while his or her family member or loved one got out of the house for a while. I noticed in the beginning the loved ones wouldn't want to leave—they'd feel too guilty. But as trust was built up, they'd start going grocery shopping or running errands, and then they would feel comfortable going to a movie or playing golf.

When my first "patient" died, I was brought in to the staff counselor to talk about the impact her death had on me. They set me up with weekly counseling sessions and grief support for six weeks. In between the sessions, I'd get a call or a card telling me that I was important to the organization and that they understood how difficult it is to lose someone with whom I had become so close in such a short time. I have never felt so treasured and loved by any organization in my life. It was an amazing experience, and it has cemented my heart with all the hospice workers and volunteers in the world. They do amazing work.

—**Kathryn M., Glen Cove, NY**

describe the job

Treating volunteers with respect and dignity is important to their happiness and the success of your nonprofit. To make their work easier and more rewarding for everyone involved, most nonprofits work out job descriptions for their volunteers. This ensures there will be no surprises that can derail a volunteer as well as a nonprofit. A volunteer job description should include:

- Length of job

- Skills required

- Reporting system: who does the volunteer report to

- Grievance system: to whom and how does the volunteer report problems?

- Other specific information to your organization or to this job, like clothing or licenses required

- Ways to record volunteer's hours once she starts

Create a book or file of all volunteer jobs with a fairly detailed description of each job. Share that job description with a potential volunteer before matching the person with the job. This ensures that the volunteer knows exactly what is being asked of her as well as training requirements, evaluation components, and reporting structure. If the volunteer needs special equipment, bonding or licensing, or drug testing, these and all special requirements should be included in the job description.

Some nonprofits find it helpful to create a volunteer agreement that volunteers sign and date. Here the nonprofit notes any special rules of the nonprofit and how volunteers are to comply. For example, an agreement may state: "I understand that I will be assigned according to the needs of the nonprofit and that I should not expect my choice of assignment." Or, "If I have concerns about any policies or procedures, I will discuss them in private with the head of volunteers."

Release of All Claims

Some nonprofits ask their volunteers to sign a release form that essentially releases the nonprofit from all claims or liability for any injuries caused by the volunteer or for any damages caused to the volunteer's property while working as a volunteer.

Confidentiality Agreements

Most problems are not with legal damages but are about breaches of confidentiality. It is important that volunteers know what can happen if they violate a client's or a donor's confidentiality. New federal regulations applying to health-care nonprofits are explicit in what constitutes a violation of privacy. There are also regulations about what information volunteers may access. For this reason, some nonprofits ask their volunteers to sign a confidentiality agreement that stipulates that all client and donor information will be kept confidential.

Some nonprofits also want their volunteers to sign an honesty pledge of sorts, which means that the volunteer will not use the nonprofit services or assets for any private gain; for example, borrowing an organization's vehicle for private use.

matching time and talent

Making it easier to volunteer

Here's the new reality of nonprofits: While many are willing to volunteer, few have the time to make a real commitment. Your big challenge is not in recruiting volunteers so much as in helping potential volunteers find the time to volunteer. How do you do this? First, break down each volunteer job into hourly, daily, or weekly portions. Even if a program is ongoing, you need to break down the tasks to manageable bites so that a volunteer can give an hour, a half day, or a day for a limited period of time. Then ask your time-stressed volunteers to work for a specific bit of time on a specific project or program. Consider pairing up volunteers in a job-share situation so they can spot each other if one can't make it to their volunteer job.

While all volunteer jobs are important—be it answering the phone or filing invoices—some call for a great deal of responsibility. Take the mail, for example. A common volunteer job is getting the mail from the mailbox or post office, opening it, photocopying the checks, entering the check amount into the computer, even writing out the deposit slip. Some even have volunteers make the deposits in the bank. This is a vulnerable position for a volunteer. What if a donation was entered incorrectly into the computer database? Or a check got lost? Do you want a volunteer to be responsible for this important income stream? At the very least, have two volunteers do this job together and act as each other's check and balance. Always plan for redundancy. Make sure you have two volunteers trained for every job. As your organization grows, you may want to hire someone to handle all these financial transactions.

Reasons to Be a Volunteer

- Meet new people.

- Make new friends.

- Learn about social issues.

- Interact with people who share your interests and passions.

- Network in your current line of work.

- Develop new skills and talents for your résumé.

- Change career directions.

- Maintain your skills during a period of layoff.

- Improve your knowledge about a particular topic.

- Dust off skills that have been dormant for a while.

- Get training that will benefit you later.

- Develop a new hobby.

- Make a unique contribution— that is, make something happen that wouldn't have been possible without you.

- Get satisfaction by knowing you're doing good work well— and have fun in the process.

FIRST PERSON SUCCESS STORY
My turning point

When my friend Ruth asked me to join the board of directors of an organization that honors heroes of the civil rights movement, I was nervous about what I was getting myself into. Although I had some writing and public relations experience, I was an accountant by trade. The board already had a treasurer, however, and I was thrust into the position of public relations expert. While I didn't think I knew that much about PR, I found I was a fast learner. In fact, before long, my story pitch about our project attracted a reporter who wrote an article on the front of the metro section of our local newspaper! I found PR so exciting that I took several classes in it, and now it's my full-time job. —Sarah F., Chicago, Il

typical volunteer jobs

Nonprofits have the same needs as any for-profit business. People are enlisted to answer the phones, keep track of the money, maintain the Web site, design brochures, sit on the board of directors, and plan annual events. Then, of course, there is the direct work volunteers do, whether organizing food drives or fundraisers, helping clients, or caring for animals in the zoo.

Most likely, this hands-on work for a good cause is what interests most volunteers. But try to "share the wealth" of your organization and ask volunteers to consider the behind-the-scenes tasks that have to be taken care of as well.

Typical Volunteer Jobs

Here are the types of volunteer positions you may find at nonprofit groups, ranging from your professional trade association to your community's food bank.

Publicity Lay out a brochure and submit it to the president, send wording of a workshop to each speaker for okay; proofread brochures, send press releases to four local papers and school newsletters.

Building-and-grounds management Submit building-use forms, coordinate scheduling of time or bus transportation for students.

Food Arrange for and coordinate food and beverages for an upcoming fundraiser with the caterer.

Telephone receptionist Answer phones, greet visitors and clients.

Records keeper and filer Keep track of mail and receipts.

Bulk mailings Stuff, seal, and sort large mailings.

ASK THE EXPERTS

Is it smart to ask volunteers to do the same skill that they use at work?

It depends. Some people feel it is only right to volunteer their hard-earned skills, be it bookkeeping or Web design or nursing. In fact, many charities need—and rely upon—people to donate their vocational skills. But don't feel bad if a volunteer declines to donate those skills. In fact, many folks get the most enjoyment from donating skills that don't otherwise get used.

Our nonprofit provides birding walks in the parks. The money we raise from this work is used to help provide food for birds in our parks. We have a number of people who are interested in working as bird walkers for us, but they don't know much about birds. What can we do?

People love to share their expertise. Consider setting up a mentoring training program. Have your qualified birders teach those who want to train to be birders. Many people volunteer to learn new skills. Take advantage of that desire if you can. It's a win-win situation for everyone.

volunteer follow-up

Just like a paid staff member, a volunteer needs to be evaluated frequently and regularly, if for no other reason than to be celebrated and rewarded frequently for meeting objectives. Often, everyone who volunteered on a specific project, for instance, gets so focused on the work that when goals are finally met, the volunteers disband and that's the end of it. A smarter way to go is to have one last meeting to talk about the project or task and discuss what was helpful and what wasn't. In short, measure their accomplishments against their efforts and then celebrate!

The Volunteer Questionnaire

When volunteers leave for any reason, ask them to fill out a form with questions like those below. Feedback will help your volunteer projects run more smoothly.

1. What did you enjoy most about your volunteer experience?

2. Did you feel your role or job was adequately explained to you?

3. What kinds of improvements could be made?

4. Did the project take up more time than you were told?

5. What message would you like to communicate to future volunteers?

6. How did your experience connect you to the mission of the project?

One sure way to find out if your volunteers are happy is to ask them to reup for the same assignment. If you get some declines, it could mean your volunteers were bored or unhappy with the work. Offer to change their jobs. There will inevitably be changes of personnel in volunteer groups, and you need to prepare for that. One way to avoid volunteer burnout is by rotating jobs and responsibilities.

How to Reward a Volunteer

Thanking volunteers is so important; yet many nonprofits forget to do this or thank them in an uninspiring, rudimentary way. How do you say thank you to someone who gives their time, talent, advice (and who often brings in cookies or treats in addition to giving their time)? First ask them how they want to be rewarded. If you draw a blank, here are some ideas:

Create a list of things/gifts/services that you or your organization could easily provide and then ask each volunteer to circle their top five ways. Here are some creative ideas:

Flowers from a garden . . . a car wash . . . a coupon for lunch at a neighborhood restaurant . . . written recognition in the newsletter . . . a birthday card . . . a photo of the volunteer with the staff . . . a thank-you breakfast with other volunteers . . . something that a board member can contribute, like a free oil change or a 25% discount at a store . . . two free movie tickets at the local theater. Get creative and have a list that you change annually.

Most volunteers want to be looked in the eyes and thanked at the end of the day. Those who say, "Please don't give me any recognition" often really want it. Be sensitive to this. Yes, some volunteers truly want to remain anonymous, but very few. Most of us want to be treated specially, with a hug, a handshake, a hand-written thank-you, and to be recognized with fellow volunteers at the annual dinner or gala or volunteer event.

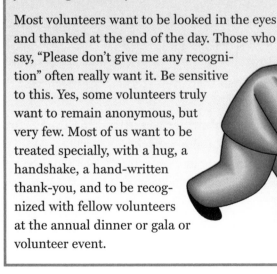

now what do I do?

Answers to common questions

We have a volunteer who I think would be great at answering the phone. But my board thinks she is too young for the job. How can answering the phone be such a big deal?

Answering the telephone is an easy job for a volunteer to fill since it seemingly requires very few skills. However, be aware that the *first* contact many people will have with your organization is the telephone answerer, so make sure that this person (or better yet, these persons) are well trained and evaluated frequently (see page 108). You don't want a major donor calling to ask for you and the volunteer not knowing how to put the phone call through or disconnecting the call without getting the donor's name.

I am the head of the board of a nonprofit we started three years ago. I love the work, but now all I seem to be doing is finding and managing volunteers. What can I do?

You might want to consider appointing a volunteer to be the director of volunteers. Give that person the job of finding, managing, evaluating, and thanking volunteers. However, keep your work as supervisor so you know what is going on.

Who should pay for background checks?

Many nonprofits, especially if they deal with such vulnerable groups as children, the disabled, or the elderly, will require volunteers to submit to a routine background check. These checks serve an important purpose: to generally screen for people who might pose a real threat to your clients. The problem is that these background checks can cost $10 to $250. To off-set that cost, you might ask prospective volunteers to pay it all or a portion of it. This will ensure that they are indeed interested in helping.

Are there any one-time volunteer opportunities that I can offer to potential time-stressed volunteers?

Are there ever! Chances are your annual fundraiser will need lots of volunteers. They can collect tickets at the door, help with food, or clean up.

A lot of parents of young children say they would love to volunteer, but they really need to spend time with their family. I understand their time constraints, but is there any way around this?

Create some volunteer jobs that involve the whole family. Popular projects for families include providing food for the hungry, visiting or helping the elderly, and cleaning up the environment. Try brainstorming volunteer ideas with a group of parents with young children—for this meeting, it might be a good idea to offer some child-care activities to keep the children occupied.

Now where do I go?

CONTACTS

www.volunteermatch.org
VolunteerMatch is a leader in the nonprofit world dedicated to helping everyone find a great place to volunteer. The organization offers a variety of online services to support a community of nonprofit, volunteer, and business leaders committed to civic engagement.

BOOKS

Barnes & Noble Basics: Volunteering
By Hope Egan

The Power Years: A User's Guide to the Rest of Your Life
By Ken Dychtwald and Daniel J. Kadlec

Make a Difference: America's Guide to Volunteering and Community Service, Revised
By Arthur I. Blaustein

Voices from the Heart: In Celebration of America's Volunteers
By Brian O'Connell

7

Public relations

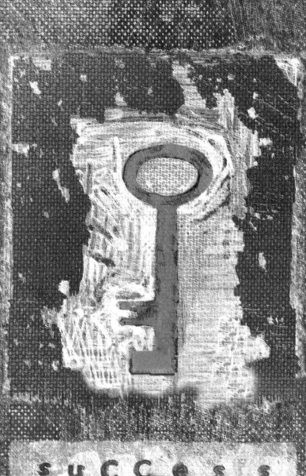

suCCess

building awareness

Great news—your program is working, and you can see a difference in your community. This is what you have been working for! This is the joy of working in the nonprofit world. Why not spread the good news around? In order for your nonprofit to become known, people need to hear of your organization. What better way than with a good story? There are a number of layers of awareness that a message has to get through in order to capture the public's attention.

The first stage of publicity is awareness. This is an ongoing need because as new people move into your area, you want to make them aware of your organization. This is also an area of great frustration for many people who have been active in an organization that is 10 or 20 years old. "I've never heard of you" is a frustrating comment to hear when you've been doing great work for so long. Accept it and use it as a teaching moment. When people are aware of you, they say things like, "Oh, I've heard of you."

The next level is understanding. "Oh, I've heard of you, and you do the following . . . " This indicates a deeper level of understanding, usually the result of brochures, newsletters, radio ads, newspaper coverage, billboards, and having heard from a friend about your organization.

The next deeper level of understanding is, "Oh, I've heard of you. You provide the following services, and you helped a friend of mine." There now is an emotional connection between the person and the organization, and you can build on this personal knowledge by asking questions about the connection.

The deepest level of connections results in the question, "How can I help?" When you are asked this question, you should be able to come up with three to five opportunities for involvement, whether giving a charitable contribution, volunteering, giving a silent auction item, or whatever you need. These are the words you long to hear, because they mean that your organization is valued.

FIRST PERSON INSIGHTS
Be Prepared to Ask

I am the board president of a service that helps homeless people access services in a one-stop-shopping method. It cuts down on their frustration and time spent shuffling from one location to another.

Our nonprofit was asked to give a talk at a lunch of local business people. I couldn't make the lunch and asked the new volunteer who heads publicity to go in my place. I gave her all our information about our organization. She was a seasoned pro, and I knew she would do just fine. And she did. In fact, she did so well that afterward she told me people were coming up to her and asking, "What can I do to help?" and "What do you need?" She said she looked like a deer in headlights. She didn't know what to ask for! I learned a big lesson. At our next meeting, I told this story and said we all had to practice simply asking for money to help fund our program. It's as simple as that. **—Alice K., Los Angeles, CA**

tell your story

Writing your nonprofit's story

Nobody knows the story of your nonprofit like you do, so the place to begin is at the very beginning. Why did you create this organization? What problem are you solving, and what was it within you that was moved enough to do something about it?

When you are telling the story, use the old nonprofit adage "hit the head, hit the heart, and hit the guts." What does this mean?

The head part means know the numbers, the return on investment, how many donors, average gift size, number of people served in the past three years, etc. Know the figures, the budget size, and all the information an engineer type or accountant type might want to know. "Head" people will want to know the statistics about your nonprofit.

The heart part means knowing the social problem you are solving, what the general needs of your clients are, why your services are helping, how your clients got to where they are, etc. Generally, people want to know that your organization is doing good and that the people who are involved in your organization are good people doing their best. "Heart" people will connect with your feelings about your work.

The guts part refers to first-person testimonials from clients whose lives have been influenced positively by your services. These stories come from person to person, thank-you notes, or through interviews with service users.

TIP: Be sure to get written consent to use these stories prior to putting them in print. The same with photographs; get permission in writing. "Guts" people will want to meet people you are helping and hear from them directly.

The Case Statement

A case statement is a document that "states the case" for supporting your organization. It is an essential document because it becomes the backbone to your grants, annual appeal text, and brochure text.

To begin, get everything down on paper. The length doesn't matter. Write about your organization, its strengths and weaknesses, threats and opportunities, plans and visions, conflicts. Include organizational charts, succession and redundancy plans, and budgets (pie in the sky and down to earth). Then share it with a very select group of people who can be trusted with confidential information. Some of the information might not be flattering to your organization, but it will show where resources and effort need to be put to strengthen your organization. This document is called the "inside case" and is seen only by an inner circle of people.

Once there is agreement on the issues reflected in the document, the "public case" for support is drafted from the inside case. It highlights the strengths, successes, and uniqueness of your organization and makes the case for why someone would make a contribution to your organization. It also discusses how the organization solves problems and responds to changes that are unexpected. This document is meant for public consumption and will be used in various ways and edited to create different documents, such as grant proposals, brochures, and appeal letters.

This process ensures that the language used to describe your organization is always the same and consistent, and that the facts and figures quoted are consistent. It also prevents someone from applying for a grant or a gift that really isn't relevant to or a priority for your organization.

the marketing plan

Communicate your story to the people

A marketing plan is a great asset to a nonprofit. It's a 12- to 18-month calendar of activities designed to build upon each other. It integrates communication techniques with various market segments inside and outside your organization.

The plan includes the newsletters, brochures, paid advertisements (all forms), the Web site updates, public-speaking engagements, cultivation events, education events, and all communications activities your organization would like to accomplish. What "target markets" do you want to communicate with? In the beginning, you might want to keep it simple and market to your volunteers, donors, prospective donors, and service users. As you grow in the ability to be more accurate in communications (or to segment your markets better), break these broad groups apart and add layers.

For example, instead of all donors, break them up into dollar segments (such as donors of $50 and less; $51 to $100 donors; $101 to $250 . . .) or geographic segments, such as neighborhoods, gated communities, ZIP codes, or subdivisions. This is the easiest and cheapest way to segment your markets.

TIP: When you create your marketing plan, go for the maximum without budgetary restrictions. You can always cut back or ask folks to make contributions to meet the budgetary needs.

Segmenting Your Market

To see how each different segment responds to your targeted mailing, run a colored marker down the side of the reply envelopes so you will know what response rate each different segment had, so you can decide whether to repeat it or not.

Whenever you speak publicly, have a response card for each guest, so you can capture their names and comments. Or better yet, hold a drawing right there for dinner for two at a local restaurant (which was donated by the restaurant) so you can gather names and contact information for those who were at the event. Then get their information into your database. Enter where they heard you, the topic, the location and date, and then send each one a handwritten follow-up note of thanks and an invitation to your next open house or special free event. Always have the next step ready to go before you have finished the first step, or "touch." It is estimated to take a minimum of seven touches to get the "how can I help?" response you want.

get their attention

Starting newsletters and other attention grabbers

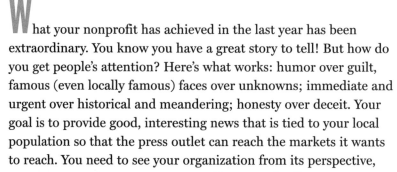

What your nonprofit has achieved in the last year has been extraordinary. You know you have a great story to tell! But how do you get people's attention? Here's what works: humor over guilt, famous (even locally famous) faces over unknowns; immediate and urgent over historical and meandering; honesty over deceit. Your goal is to provide good, interesting news that is tied to your local population so that the press outlet can reach the markets it wants to reach. You need to see your organization from its perspective,

not yours. For example, if you want to get on television, make the opportunities visual. A group of children in matching T-shirts doing something is much more interesting visually than a group of adults around a table making decisions. Think like a camera lens.

If you want radio attention, make your message sound good and interesting. Find a great voice among your volunteers, play music, or have the children's choir sing behind the voiceover.

Want press attention? Write the story of your organization yourself and prepare a fact sheet. When a disaster happens and you are the expert, call the reporter who covers nonprofits or your area of service and help him with background information and whatever else he may need. Be his resource, and you will be remembered when you need to get a story about your nonprofit covered.

Write guest editorials. Ask your volunteers to write letters to the editor. Get creative!

Your Web Site

Potential donors and volunteers who surf the Web will want to know that you have a Web site. It adds legitimacy in their minds. So how do you get one? If you have a volunteer who can design Web sites or can afford to have a paid Web master create your site, go for it.

First determine three names you might want to operate under. (See page 30 for registering your name.)

As you work to build your site, always include how you can be reached: a direct e-mail to you, where you operate, the hours, the telephone and fax numbers. Also have your mission statement and other relevant visionary language on the site. The final information you want is how people can access your services, how people can volunteer to help your service users, and, most important of all, how people can donate to your nonprofit.

Update your Web site regularly (okay, as often as you can) with good news, the latest gift or success, the next event and photos of the last event showing how much fun it was. But if you do not have the capability to update the site, don't put time-sensitive information on it. When information is outdated and not updated, your organization will look slack and will be perceived as less than capable.

now what do I do?
Answers to common questions

I have heard that a lot of nonprofits are using the Internet to raise money. How does that work?

If you have a Web site, talk to your designer about setting up a feature so you can accept most credit cards. You have to have a bank or credit card business set you up with the ability to accept cards. Then have your Web site designer set up the required secure fields on your site. It will cost you more not to take plastic than to take it. Why? Because the average contribution on a credit card is far higher than the average check written to a nonprofit. And the majority of Americans have made a purchase on the Web, so they are used to following the procedures. In fact, the members of the younger generation only want to use their cards (they never carry cash according to statisticians) and the older generation wants to get frequent flyer miles to see their grandchildren.

My nonprofit helps take care of abused animals. Can we approach members of the local ASPCA and ask them to mention us in their newsletter?

Yes. Contact them and ask for a meeting with their decision makers. Lay out what you would like from them and what you are willing to offer them and see if there is a mutual need and a desire to assist. Don't worry if they turn you down. Ask them what they need to see from your organization for them to change their minds. When you meet their expectations, go back and ask again.

How do we evaluate the effectiveness of our marketing plan?

Because nonprofits have no "bottom line" against which to measure their success, they need to be creative in assessing how well their marketing programs are working. One way to determine effectiveness is to always ask prospective donors how they heard about your organization. If you are doing a fundraising mailing, for instance, ask donors to check the appropriate box if they heard about you from the radio or the newspaper or the Internet or word of mouth. If you see a rise in the radio responses, then you know your marketing ads on the radio are working.

One of our board members is very involved in the mayor's race for re-election. She wants us to mention how the mayor has helped us in our newsletter. Can we do that?

This is a sensitive area and one in which you should proceed cautiously. It is wholly appropriate to state in your newsletter how supportive the city has been. It is a different matter to state how helpful an elected official has been. You should not get involved in the politics of the situation, but as with all donors, you should give credit and recognition where credit is due. Just remember that for as many people who love the current political leader, there are probably the same number of people who oppose the politician. So stay out of politics and stay focused on your mission and those you serve.

Now where do I go?

BOOKS

Promoting Issues and Ideas
By M. Booth & Associates
General guidebook on public relations, which includes a chapter on special events and covers such issues as staffing, materials, invitations, equipment, and follow-up.

CPR: Creative Strategies for Successful Fundraising, Marketing, Communications, and Management
By Alvin H. Reiss
Presents case studies that offer accessible, adaptable strategies for dealing with a broad range of nonprofit concerns, and includes a chapter on special events.

Selling Goodness: The Guerrilla P.R. Guide to Promoting Your Charity, Nonprofit Organization, or Fund-Raising Event
By Michael Levine
Encourages nonprofits to learn public relations from the corporate world and to promote their causes vigorously through newspaper, radio, and television venues, and public speaking.

Planning Special Events
By James S. Armstrong
Practical guide to conducting special events and incorporating them into a fundraising program. Explains how to determine the needs of the organization, select the type of event, choose the best location, create a budget, market the event, take advantage of follow-up activities, and measure and analyze the results of the project. Includes sample planning worksheets.

Cash Now! A Manual of Twenty-nine Successful Fundraising Events
By Aaron Franks and Norman E. Franks
Detailed descriptions of twenty-nine different ideas for special events. Scope includes publicity and promotion, equipment and personnel requirements and suggestions for future "spinoff" activities.

Raising Big Bucks: The Complete Guide to Producing Pledge-based Special Events
By Cindy Kaitcer
Focuses on the planning and evaluation of pledge-based events as profitable fundraisers for nonprofit organizations.

8
Finding funding

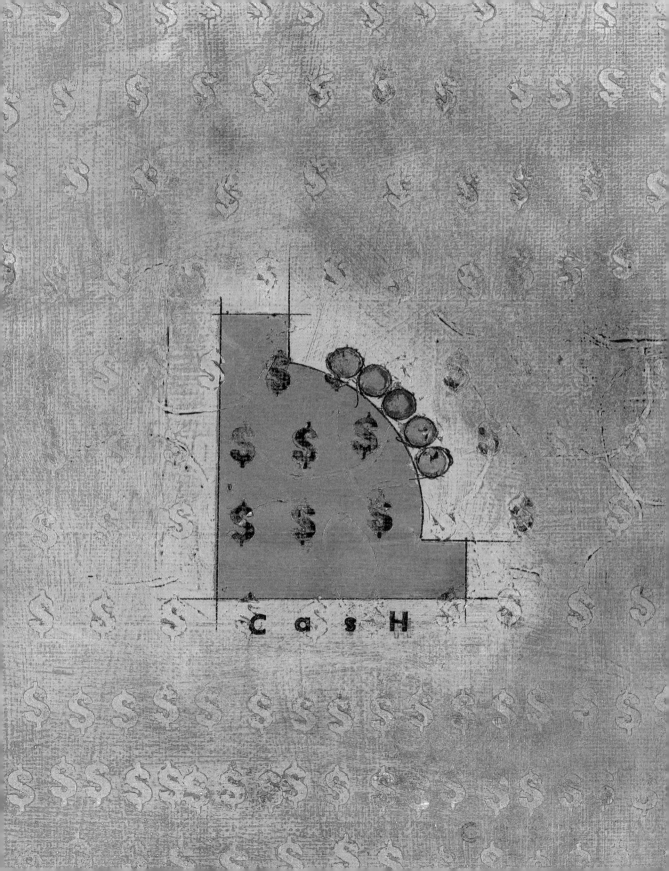

who gives and why

Americans are generous donors

It's the big question every nonprofit volunteer wants the answer to. Who gives the most money? When it comes to giving money to charities, individuals give the most money. Typically, donors give first to their faith organization of choice, then to schools, colleges or universities, and then to health-care agencies or hospitals. After those Big Three, donors tend to make smaller gifts to many organizations with whom they are personally affiliated; for example, a nonprofit that helped with a family member.

Why do faith-based organizations receive the most money, followed by education and health care? Because these three types of institutions have been asking for money longer than newer types of nonprofit organizations such as environmental and arts organizations. While start-ups typically have a more difficult time raising money than established ones, once in business for between five and seven years, most nonprofits are able to compete with the more established nonprofits for donor dollars.

Here is some good news: Your first layer of donors will most likely be your neighbors, friends, work colleagues, and all the folks in your world, especially those who are volunteering at your nonprofit.

TIP: Most people who volunteer give a larger gift (when asked) than those who do not volunteer.

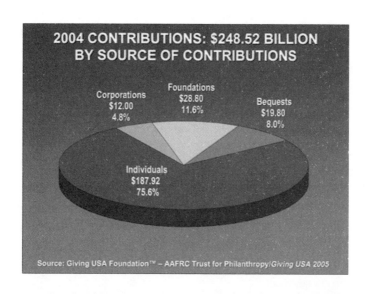

2004 CONTRIBUTIONS: $248.52 BILLION BY SOURCE OF CONTRIBUTIONS

Corporations $12.00 4.8%
Foundations $28.80 11.6%
Bequests $19.80 8.0%
Individuals $187.92 75.6%

Source: Giving USA Foundation™ – AAFRC Trust for Philanthropy/*Giving USA 2005*

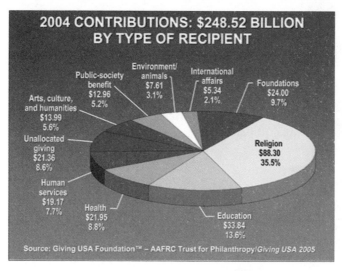

2004 CONTRIBUTIONS: $248.52 BILLION BY TYPE OF RECIPIENT

Public-society benefit $12.96 5.2%
Environment/animals $7.61 3.1%
International affairs $5.34 2.1%
Foundations $24.00 9.7%
Arts, culture, and humanities $13.99 5.6%
Unallocated giving $21.36 8.6%
Religion $88.30 35.5%
Human services $19.17 7.7%
Health $21.95 8.8%
Education $33.84 13.6%

Source: Giving USA Foundation™ – AAFRC Trust for Philanthropy/*Giving USA 2005*

in-kind donations

Another way to keep your nonprofit going

Yes, money is always welcomed, but so, too, are donations that show heart. These donations are gifts of things, services, advice, time, and talents. They are known as in-kind donations, and they can often make or break a nonprofit. For example, you are having an outdoor fundraiser and you want to provide water and soda at this event. Your local soda-pop bottler might be willing to give you 10 cases of drinks for your event, but he can't give you $100 for the event. Does the soda save you money by taking that off the shopping list? Then it is a great gift.

In-kind services might be an accountant offering you 10 hours of free accounting per month. The accountant cannot take that gift of time as a tax deduction or as a charitable gift, but it can save your organization money so you won't have to pay an accountant for these services.

In-kind gifts can be a great help to organizations, especially when just starting out. Where in-kind gifts are not helpful is when an organization, business, or person wants to give you something you don't want or can't use but still wants recognition for the "gift."

TIP: Create a gift acceptance committee of the board. This committee will review gifts of questionable value to decide if they can be received or if they have to be declined.

Types of In-kind Gifts

Want in-kind or noncash contributions that will help your organization? Get creative and add to the list:

- Day sponsorship ads on public radio stations

- Car wash coupons (to give to your loyal volunteers)

- Free insert in your local newspaper (to promote your cause)

- Flowers or plants from the local nursery or floral shop

- One hour a week from a professional

- Billboards at the nonprofit rate, or for free if they are in obscure locations

- Day-old breads and pastries from a local coffee shop or local franchise

- Service work from local college seniors

- Clothes, furniture, equipment, books, etc.

types of grants

There is a whole
buffet of grants
out there

Great, your nonprofit has a big project in need of funding. And it looks as if getting a grant would be just the ticket. But before you go rushing off to write your proposal and mail it to the world of foundations, know this: There are many different types of grants, and one size does not fit all. Here is a list of basic grant types. When you find the type that best matches your project, then you can start writing. (For more on getting a grant, see Chapter 10.)

Program grants The money is used for a specific program, such as establishing a girls' softball team. This type is most common for group projects, especially for nonprofit organizations.

Continuing support grants While most program grants are made for one year only, some are renewed for another year.

Start-up grants Also known as program-development grants, this money is given to provide initial support for a project but not fund it entirely. Start-up grants (sometimes called seed money) help bring in more grants by showing other prospective donors a base of support.

Research grants These funds pay to study an issue, such as a cure for a disease. The grant money is often funneled through an institution, such as a hospital or university, which provides the research facilities and pays the salaries of the professional and research staff.

Scholarship grants and fellowships These grants cover expenses for undergraduate, graduate, or postgraduate education. They can be awarded to individuals or to institutions that pass them on to individuals. Graduate and postgraduate grants may be classified as fellowships.

Challenge or matching grants These grants boost contributions by requiring that part of a project's funding come from other sources, such as new donors or other grants.

Endowments Established with individual monetary gifts and sometimes grants, endowments are invested to provide a continuous flow of interest income to support the cause. Large endowments are the best way to maintain a nonprofit organization.

Consulting grants Donors may pay for hiring a consultant on a project.

Conference grants Grant funds may be made available to set up and run conferences or seminars, or to send project officers to such meetings.

ASK THE EXPERTS

Why is so little grant money available to cover operating costs, such as salaries or overhead expenses?

Most grantmakers prefer to help start a project or give it a boost partway through, but not to cover any ongoing expenses once it is up and running. That is because most funders feel that once a project is started, its running costs should come from other efforts, such as endowments or annual events.

I met someone recently who writes grant proposals for a living. How can this one job function expand into an entire job?

When the stakes are high, a professional grant writer can easily earn his or her salary. Big nonprofit organizations often keep several grant proposal writers on staff or on retainer to target the right donors for specific projects and tailor proposals to win funding.

asking donors

Because individuals give so much, start with them first. If you can, meet with known donors in person. Usually individual donors will give you a lot of cues and clues about their wealth and interests if you observe, research, and ask them. Are they eager to talk about their philanthropic passions? Is their name in every arts program and play-bill? At what amount? Look for their interest or inclination to give to your type of charity and then, specifically, your charity. And look for their ability to contribute large gifts, especially bequests.

The old adage in fundraising is called the Rule of Rights: You want to have the right person/Ask the right prospect/For the right amount of money/For the right purpose/At the right time. So begin your fundraising not in the mail or through the newsletter—these are passive forms of asking for contributions—but face-to-face with your friends and neighbors and see the larger gifts begin to come the more you ask. Get folks to actually see what you are doing and how lives are being changed, and they'll be asking you, "How can I help?"—four of the most beautiful words you'll ever hear. Then you can ask for money, stuff, time, advice, prayers, or whatever else you need and want.

Note: It is important to keep accurate information about your donor and her gifts over the years to your organization. You need to note the date of gift, date of thank you and receipt; amount; form of the gift (check, cash, stock, life insurance policy, etc.); purpose of the gift if it was restricted; whether the donor attended fundraisers and if so, with whom she sat, with whom she spoke, what she particularly liked. You also want to collect information about donors of yours who have given to other organizations. What other organizations do they support or volunteer for or whose boards do they sit on? All this information is to be kept confidential and treated with great discretion.

Phases of Development

Phase 1
Prospecting: the who
Lists of names from your Rolodex, your friends' Christmas card lists, worker colleagues . . .

Phase 2
Qualifying: the how much
Rating and screening how much someone might be able to give to your organization.

Phase 3
Cultivating: getting to know you
Come see what we are doing, how we are doing it, and the lives that are being improved.

Phase 4
Soliciting
This is where you specifically state what "a gift in the amount of $_____ would do to help keep our work going."

Phase 5
Stewarding-cultivating
Thanking the donor for their gifts and spending their contributions the way they asked you to spend it; or reporting how you used their money prior to asking for the next gift.

corporate donors

They often give to
those organizations
where their employees
volunteer

Corporate donors are often keen to give to nonprofits, especially those in their community. Before you can effectively ask for money, you need to know why corporations give money away.

Corporations give for three major reasons:

- They have to give money away in order to retain their charitable status for their own corporate foundation.

- They want publicity for being a good corporate citizen.

- They want to benefit the communities in which their employees work, live, and play.

What do corporations want to give to? Often they will give money to support areas of study that relate to their products, like the Westinghouse Scholars program or the GE Science Fair prizes. They will often sponsor events in which their employees are active or playing leadership roles. And they will give money to start-up programs or projects. Most corporations do not want to fund capital campaigns or make ongoing annual gifts that support maintaining projects or annual operations.

Corporate Gifts Out of the Box

In-kind donations

This kind of giving is a specialty of corporations, whether they're Fortune 500 companies or simple mom-and-pop stores. Instead of money, companies offer to supply goods to assist your project. Furnishings, computers, medicine, food, even empty offices are just a few possible in-kind benefits you might want to request. The

type of assistance often depends on the products the company produces. Consider the equipment your project will require, then look for a local corporation or retail business as a possible source.

Technical assistance

Many corporations offer their employees time to participate in philanthropic causes. For example, an after-school tutoring program might need advice on maintaining its buses. Mechanics employed by a local company could spend an afternoon a week to help solve mechanical problems.

help from other nonprofits

The value of civic group memberships

There is a special bond among those who work in the nonprofit world. They share a common goal of wanting to help others. That's why it is so important for your nonprofit to turn to its fellow non-profiters for support. Think of those local civic groups that are right in your backyard. Groups such as the Kiwanis, the Episcopal Church Women, Rotary Clubs, and Hadassah, to name just a few, exist to serve others. Your nonprofit might be just the cause they are looking for. Usually these gifts are small, but again they can add great value to the public's perception of your organization.

For example, suppose the Lions Club's members are particularly concerned with eye care and eye disease prevention. It might be helpful for your organization, which has eye-care programs, to call the president of the Lions Club and ask if you can be a speaker at one of their monthly meetings. You can speak and show slides about what your programs are doing to help others, and you can hand out literature about your organization. In addition, you can recruit volunteers for your board or programs. Ask the Lions Club if you can publicize the event, especially if the club makes a contribution. That way you both get public recognition!

Your Nonprofit Portfolio

Have copies of these documents on hand to show to donors, civic groups, and foundations:

■ Governing documents: code of ethics/statement of values, standards of practice, operation or accountability, including conflict-of-interest and affirmative action or other inclusiveness policies

■ List of board members and officers, their terms, occupations, and contact information

■ Long-range plans, vision and mission statements

■ Most recent financial audit report

■ Any ongoing evaluation procedures for assessing effectiveness of the organization, employees, managers and trustees, and programs

■ Current IRS form 990 (including all parts and schedules except contributors list with amounts, which is protected under the Privacy Act)

■ Bylaws and operating guidelines for the board of directors

borrowing from banks

First, make sure
you can pay it
back

Borrowing money from banks is also a way to raise money. But just like your for-profit colleagues, you will have to pay back the loan with interest. Banks don't discount the interest rate because you are doing good things for the community.

Applying for a bank loan is just like applying for a business loan or a mortgage; you have to have good credit, assets that can be used as collateral, and a repayment plan. Many banks will not loan money to a new organization; they want to see that you have a proven record of spending within your budgetary means and want to see that others within the community are willing to invest their money in your work. Start-ups can't show that kind of track record.

Sometimes a large donor or a wealthy member of the board will be willing to co-sign a loan for your organization. This can be very helpful to get that building construction started so you can gather more support from other donors. But it can also put you in a weak position where you feel responsible to this person. What if this co-signer wants your organization to hire his niece? How would you feel about saying no to this very important person? Or what if he wants you to name the new building for a member of his family who you know had less than a great reputation?

Having the organization so reliant on one person can be compromising for the board and leave vulnerable those being served by the agency. So consider borrowing only when you are certain your non-profit can secure the loan.

ASK THE EXPERTS

What do we need to do to qualify for a loan?

To qualify for a loan, an organization must be a nonprofit 501(c)(3) organization, incorporated, and have at least three years of operating history. You also need to have an independent board of directors with at least five unrelated members. You must be able to submit monthly financial statements and cash-flow projections, just as a for-profit would. Moreover, you must be able to show the ability in the future to repay the loan.

We are at our wits' end. Can we borrow to cover a cash-flow crunch?

Yes. There are actually good reasons to borrow money, such as having pledges from donors who haven't paid them as yet. Under the right circumstances, a loan can stabilize cash flow so your services are not jeopardized during cash-poor times. The ability to borrow money is often just what is needed to bring financial equilibrium to a nonprofit at the mercy of unpredictable income streams, growing service demands, or outdated equipment.

online fundraising

The Internet is a big source for funding

There are several ways to raise money online. If your nonprofit already has a Web site established, you can arrange to accept donations online. This means you will need to be able to accept credit cards. Yes, there is a processing fee you will have to pay when credit cards get involved, but it is worth it. The money you can raise online will offset the processing fees because you will pay the fee only when there is a transaction. fundraising: shopping online, which results in a gift to the nonprofit of your choice, and accepting credit-card gifts on your favorite charity's Web site.

Another popular option is to arrange for indirect donations from other Web sites, typically brandname stores which have online Web sites. These web stores often contribute a small percentage of what a buyer purchases to a nonprofit. Sometimes those nonprofits are preselected, but in many cases, the choice of charity is left to the buyer to select. You want to make sure your donors are aware that when they shop at their favorite brandname Web sites they can be contributing to your nonprofit. All they need to do is go through these Web sites which act as online portals before they shop:

www.thegreatergood.com

www.buyforcharity.com

Online Commerce

Is your organization capable of selling a product in a shop or online that can increase and diversify your income streams? It is a valuable idea to examine closely before you take the plunge.

For example, say that a mental health organization provides a fun, stimulating atmosphere in which developmentally and mentally challenged individuals can learn work skills, play board games, exercise, and learn how to grow plants and flowers.

The club "members" decide they want to sell their plants and hand-made aprons and pot holders. They want the proceeds from the sales to be divided 50–50 between program expansion and the members themselves. Everyone who grows or makes items for sale will receive an equal share of 50% of that month's profits. Is this allowable?

Yes, it is. But the income from the sales will be taxed at regular rates for the members, and the 50% profits might be taxed as unrelated sales. Check with your accountant or financial adviser to determine whether it will be worth your organization undertaking a for-profit venture. As more and more organizations do it (like art schools selling the art of their students), expect the federal government and the IRS to scrutinize this activity more and more in the future.

now what do I do?
Answers to common questions

I have never raised money, and I hate to ask people for anything. I don't even know how to begin. What do I do?

Choosing the prospect

There is no correct prospect for you other than the ones you are most comfortable with. If you prefer to call on people you don't know, fine. If you prefer to call on friends, fine. Just let the Executive Director (ED) know on whom you plan to call and when, so he can make sure no one else is calling on that prospect.

Choosing your teammate

Even God told Noah to take the animals two by two—don't go alone! It helps keep your courage high and helps get the complete story told if two of you go together. There will be special cases when you should go alone, and that is okay, but it should not be the norm. Find a friend and make some dates to tell the story of your organization.

Making the call to get the appointment

Often this is where the "call" can go wrong. People may not want to see you, because they already know what they want to give. Ask if you may come anyway. Tell them you want the practice, and if they promise not to give less after you make the call, you'd like to come to hear about their commitment to the organization (or some other wording with which you are comfortable).

Getting the face-to-face meeting

Where is not important, as long as the prospect chooses the place. Some people prefer their office, some their home, some a restaurant. The less public, the more private the conversation, usually. But let the prospective donors decide the time and place. If they don't care, you should go to their homes to learn more about them and their interests.

Preparing for the appointment

You and your teammate need to decide who will start the conversation and how and who will say what. After two or three calls together, you'll have it down.

The visit

Breathe deeply. Remember you are asking on behalf of others, not yourself. This is meant to be a personal, meaningful, and important meeting, so there is no such thing as small talk. It is a wonderful opportunity to get together, learn more about each other, hear what is important to the prospect, and figure out together how their needs and goals and beliefs can be honored through a gift to your organization. Most visits should last less than one hour, but be aware of cues that the prospect wants you to stay or go.

Five tips for making "the ask"

1. Make them smile.

2. Make them say yes to something.

3. Ask for their advice on something.

4. Give them something that makes them feel ahead of you.

5. Ask for what you want. Be specific and concrete. Give them a time frame.

Immediately after the visit

In the car on the way home, the person not driving should write the thank-you note, thanking the prospect for his or her time and thoughtfulness. Put it on personal letterhead or note cards.

Then write your call report—your notes about the visit, what you talked about, the concerns and worries and dreams and goals of the prospect, and all follow-up steps you have committed to. Give the call report to the office. These are confidential but will serve as guides for the donor's pledge or next steps.

The next day or later after the visit

Call the office and report on the visit, relay what you asked for and what the next steps are. Mail your thank-you note if you haven't already done so.

Following up

Do whatever you committed to doing—schedule a tour, get more information, pick up their pledge card, call on the day you mutually agreed to in order to pick up their pledge.

9

Planning a special fundraising event

identifying the goals

Your nonprofit is growing by leaps and bounds. Terrific! It's time to consider doing a special event. For one thing, it's a great way to get to know people better, and better still, it is a great way to let them get to know you and your organization better. Events are good for rubbing elbows with other people and for having fun. If you want to raise money through the event, it can be done, but it is much quicker and easier to ask a few people for larger gifts than to put on a special event.

Having said that, let's look at how to make an event the best it can be.

An event can:

- Raise awareness of your organization or a special program
- Motivate the staff, the volunteers, the board of directors
- Bond folks to the institution because they are having fun
- Add cachet to your organization
- Gather press and lots of public attention
- Upset some people that their contributions are going to "fun" when the budget is tight
- Drain volunteers and staff with lots of overtime and details
- Cost more money than it makes—not just net "zero" but cost the organization money
- Help you socially set up the next step for the face-to-face visit or "ask"

An event doesn't:

- Offer intimacy
- Give much quality uninterrupted time with your donors
- Offer time to make a solicitation for a gift
- Always make money

Your Development Plan
(Events should generally be less than 10% of your fundraising goal)

Annual Fundraising Goal:	FY 2005–2006
Individuals	<u>75–80%</u>
Current Board Members	15%
Former Board members	5%
Events	10%
Face-to-face meetings	50%
Foundations	<u>20–25%</u>
Community	
Private/family	
Corporations and Business	<u>5–10%</u>

planning the event

**When you know your
goals, the rest will follow**

What do you want to accomplish by having an event? If the number one answer is to raise money, fine. But fill in the dollar amount. What are your other goals? This is an important question so you can make sure that you achieve your goals and so that you can set up the next steps for cultivation, education, or solicitation.

The second goal should be to get publicity, press, and some sort of increased image in the community. Since this is the single thing an event can do for you, it better be a goal and not some hoped-for fringe benefit.

The third goal should be to attract contributions from a market segment that likes to find events or to attract a contributing segment that wants to be seen in order to make a contribution. So be specific when you state your goals. Here is a sample goal list for an event held by a nonprofit in Hendersonville, NC.

Goals of Our Fall Event

1. To gross over $35,000 (with 250 attendees and $10,000 minimum in sponsorships)

2. To have print articles in all local papers:
   - *Hendersonville Times News*
   - *Asheville Citizen Times*
   - *Every Woman Gives* Journal

3. To have at least one television story on WWTR, WGPT, and WMGR

4. To announce the event on local public radio stations five times or more: WMLE, WMMJ, and WKAT

5. To have:
   - 20+ attendees from Stockman Hedges neighborhood
   - 10+ attendees from First National Bank and Trust
   - 10+ attendees who are also members of the Junior League and/or Women Helping Women Group

6. To get the attention of (if not the appearance of) our local celebrity Andie McDowell

7. As a result of new interest, to set up tours of the facility for at least 25 people

8. To recruit three new prospective board members

9. To increase the enthusiasm for our organization

10. To have a good time

A Checklist to Discuss with Party People

Event Timing

- Based on our goals, when is the best time to have this event?
- When are other events in our community?
- When and what are the natural highs and lows of our community?
- What are the vacation and business workloads of our staff?

Location

- Where is the best place to hold it?
- Who will be attracted?
- Who will feel uncomfortable?

Budget

- What is the best price to charge for it? At what price will people be too scared to attend? At what price will people be attracted to attend? Can we offer the event at two or three ticket prices, and if so, what will the largest donors get that the smallest donors won't?
- What is the real cost, even if we are going to get in-kind contributions to offset the cost?
- Who are the best sponsors/underwriters for this event?

Volunteer Team

- Who is the best organizer of it?
- Whose names need to be listed on the planning committee to attract attendees?

creating a budget

The event should pay for itself and then some

Once you have chosen your theme, decided on the guest list, determined the location, and set the date, you need to figure out if you can fund it. For this, you need to create a budget for the event. How will you pay for it?

The goal is for the event to pay for itself with money left over for your programs. Organizations that have established a signature event or that have more money at their disposal often feel it is more effective to pay for the event. They solicit high-level sponsorships or gifts from businesses or banks or companies that can afford to buy a table and who will want their name associated with the event.

You can also fund it through in-kind donations. This requires that you and your volunteers, board members, and staff solicit contributions of time, food, publicity, refreshments, and entertainment. Many smaller or newer organizations determine that it will be better to get to know people if they go door to door asking for gifts of food, wine, raffle items, etc., in order to get the word out person-to-person; this technique is extremely labor intensive but has the advantage of getting your organization's story told accurately by people who have been trained to tell the story.

Either way is fine, but make sure that your organization matches its people's skills, talent, and availability with the most important tasks.

TIP: Be careful. Burn-out on events can be high because there are so many details to attend to in order to make it spectacular. And whether it is a barbecue or a gala, you want your event to be so well run and smooth that it seems as though it happened magically.

Questions to Consider Before Making a Commitment to Doing the Event

- Who is going to be invited: strategically determine your markets or market segments.

- What is the tone of the event? China or plastic? Linen or paper? Black and white or riotous color?

- What time will it start and end? Will there be speakers? At what time and for how long? Who will be speaking (and do we know that they can attend)? Who will write their remarks?

- Will there be additional fundraising at the event, like a raffle or door prizes or silent auction or live auction? Are these legal in our state?

- Will there be a photographer? Will people receive the photographs for free or will they be asked to pay for them?

- How will the food be served? Buffet style, plated and served? Will we need silverware, or will it be finger food?

- Where will bars be set up? Will there be drink tickets, or will alcohol be charged per drink? Will soft drinks be free? What does our insurance policy say about serving liquor?

- Will there be a printed program for the evening, or will there be a spokesperson who thanks the sponsors? Will there be table tents thanking the sponsors?

- Will there be posters and signs up around the room telling the story of what we do and how we do it? Will clients be invited to attend? Will they receive complimentary tickets? Will staff have to pay to attend?

- Do we need to rent Port-A-Potties? Is the signage for the restrooms, exits, and parking clear?

- Is the venue handicapped accessible, and does that matter to us? Do we need a sign-language interpreter?

- And finally, who will send thank-you notes to those who attended, and what will the follow-up be once we have interested people in what we are doing?

getting to the details

Personalizing the invitations

So now you have determined your date, your theme, the ticket prices, and how many tickets will need to be sold at what level in order to achieve your fundraising goal. Great! So it is time to get to the heart of the event itself: making sure people come.

Start with the invitations. After you have determined the tone and the guest list, the invitation design should echo the flavor and tone of the event. Have the outer envelopes hand-addressed by people with neat handwriting. Ask each board member to add a personal note on the invitation front to their friends. You can have special times in your office for board note making and serve drinks and refreshments to make the chore more fun.

The volunteers can stuff and sort, seal and stamp the invitations, and the initial database should be set up with the names of all who will receive an invitation. As responses come in, over the phone or by reply card, the information about how many people will be attending, their accurate first names, how the response was received, on what date, and how much they paid for the tickets should be entered into your database. If a board member put a note on the invitation, the board member should be told that this person will be attending.

As the date of the event approaches and you haven't heard from a number of people, it is common courtesy to call the nonrespondents if the event is formal. If it is a barbecue and you want to know and have the time to call everyone, go for it. But most organizations will not call the entire list for an informal event, because the number doesn't really matter. Figure that 5% who didn't respond will attend and 10% of those who said they will attend won't. You can always ask staff and board members to eat last if more people show up than you expected.

Timing Is Everything

The timing of an event is important and becoming more and more difficult to get "right." Why? So many more organizations are holding events that the social calendar of a mid- to-small-sized community is getting crowded. First of all, check with as many other major organizations as possible to determine when their signature events will be held. There is no reason to compete if you don't have to.

Then check to see if your "industry" has a natural time for an event; for example, October is Breast Cancer Prevention month and November is national Hospice month. So these are great natural time periods for these organizations to host a showcase event. Try to avoid Christmas, Thanksgiving, and Hanukkah, as those weekends and evenings are so crowded. Many communities have important United Way campaigns that run for a few months in the fall, and they have black-out periods during which recipient agencies may not raise money. Call your United Way to find out what these dates are. And then plan with the weather, the amount of light in the day, the age of your guests, their transportation preferences, and overlay the various school schedules, and you will figure out how few "good" dates there are for an event.

But as soon as you figure out those times that work, pick one that best matches your needs for cash flow or fits with your staff availability and workloads. Then get a save-the-date postcard out as soon as you have the date, time, and place, in order to get your desired guests' attention.

event timetable

A sample event
timetable

Date	Activity
Begin	Have meeting to set goals for event
11 to 12 weeks prior	Recruit planning committee members
9 weeks prior	Reserve location
	Develop budget
	Determine objectives

Use the event as an opportunity to pull in board members, clients, staff, and other volunteers who have skills but who haven't been too active in your organization or with whom you want to become more familiar.

8 to 10 weeks prior	Get sponsors, list them on invitations
	Input lists and cross-check for errors, duplications

Set theme for the event that will run in the invitation, brochure, or information handout, possibly even the decorations and name tags.

6 weeks prior	Invitations printed and (hand) addressed with personal notes from peers
4 to 5 weeks prior	Mail invitations Use real stamps if possible
2 weeks prior	RSVPs due
	Give caterers the number of people

Gather invitation lists from board members, staff, clients; consider including neighbors, elected officials, people who can help further your cause.

Date	Activity
1 week prior	Press release sent out
2 to 3 days prior	Calls to media to remind them of event
	Calls to the VIPs from whom you have not heard
	Board members are assigned to talk with two or three VIPs
	They must call the next day and report details of the conversation for the database or write a call report
	Will there be welcoming remarks? By whom? When?
	Are there small gifts for the guests?
	Be prepared to answer how to make out the check
The day of the event	Write name tags with special marks for board members, clients, and others
	Check that guest book is in place
	Check to be sure greeters/hosts and hostesses are coming
	Check food, drinks (nonalcoholic options if alcohol is being served)
	Check plates, utensils, napkins, tablecloths
	Check that brochures are in place
	Check flowers
	Check sound system and music
	Check tour schedule of your organization and that set times are arranged with designated tour guides

tax deductions

What is and isn't tax deductible

Okay, you are almost there. But before you print the invitations, be sure to determine the tax-deductible portion of the event "cost." To do this make a good-faith estimate of what a comparable event would cost on an average day/night in a similar setting. The **fair-market value** (or FMV) of the event is then deducted from the price of the ticket, and the remaining amount is the contributed portion that attendees get to deduct from their taxes. (The only way a donor can deduct the entire ticket price is to return the unused ticket to the host organization for resale.)

How do you figure the cost of the band, the flowers, the entertainment, the party favors? Make a reasonable guess as to how much these things cost and pro rate them over the number of guests and add it to the cost of the event. Next consider the food. If the FMV of the food is $66 and the cost of the band and add-ons is $8; that's a total of $74. Thus, the deduction for each $100-a-plate donor is $26. It is your responsibility to put this information on the invitation. But check with your secretary of state's office for specific regulations for your state, because some states require certain type size and placement on the invitation. At a minimum, it must be on the receipt given to the donors.

FIRST PERSON INSIGHTS

It's all in the details

I work as a fundraiser for a college, and we were in a major capital campaign. There was a donor we had no idea how to get in front of; all our connections were really flimsy and seemed far-fetched.

So we held a dinner party in New York City and invited this alum to attend. We were very excited because she accepted the invitation. We figured out where we would seat her and who would talk with her. It turned out she attended the function because she had been in the college singing group as a student and on the invitation we had announced that the entertainment would be provided by the current singing group from campus. The choral group was wonderful. They sang upbeat show tunes, and everyone was smiling and really enjoying the music. And the next day our hard-to-reach donor called the college president announcing she wanted a tour of campus in order to learn more about the capital campaign. She made a huge gift, and music was the key to the success! We never could have guessed that. Next time I'll do more in-depth research on prospective donors.

—Sam H., Louisville, KY

evaluations

Do an after-party critique

So how did things go? Was it fun? Did you raise money? Did you get to know some of your donors better? Do you have the next steps established with them to come see what your nonprofit does? If yes, you had a great event. But do you want to do it again next year or in six months? Here is how you can decide that.

What were your goals? Were they achieved? Did you get the number of guests that you set out to have? Did you get the dollar amount you planned to net? These are quantitative questions that demand quantitative answers. Then there are the qualitative questions:

- What went well?
  - What didn't go well?
    - What would we repeat next year?
    - Will we do this event again next year?
    - What will we add? Change? Improve?
    - Who has offered to help out next year?
    - Who had a great time and might be on the brainstorming committee?
    - Who had a great time and who will approach donors so we can use their photos on our next newsletter?

Your Event Notebook

Make a three-ring binder complete with a sample invitation. Include the following:

The guest list

The list of those who attended

Those who said they would attend and who didn't show

Those who planned to attend and didn't show but who called to tell you

Who sat next to whom and enjoyed the experience

Who sat next to whom and had a dreadful time

Observations: What information the board members learned about their companions, and all other observations the committee can remember

Include budget projections and actual costs

Include the list of prospective volunteers and volunteers who actually worked on the event

Also, put in photos of how the bars were set up, what the table decorations looked like, what the favors were and where they were purchased, who provided the entertainment, and every budget expense. This way, if you decide to try this event again or something similar, the next chair will not have to reinvent the wheel and can use prior knowledge.

now what do I do?
Answers to common questions

This will be our sixth year doing our annual fundraising dinner and live auction. It's a lot of work, and as president, I am finding that a lot of the volunteers who worked on it last year are begging off helping this year. What is going on?

There could be a number of things going on, but you need to get to the bottom of it quickly. Look at the notes from last year's dinner and auction. Who had a good time? Who didn't? How did your volunteers feel after the event? Did you get their feedback? Did you celebrate their contributions? It could also be a sign that you need to come up with a new fundraising idea that will get the sparkle back in your volunteers. Start asking for suggestions.

We are having difficulty finding the time to keep detailed financial records for our event. We would all just rather do the work. Why is bookkeeping so important?

Bookkeeping is vitally important to an event, because it is the only way you can determine how cost-effective it was. There is no point in doing the work of a special event if it turns out to be cost-prohibitive. It will also show you where you are wasting money. If keeping your books is overwhelming you, then you should consider taking some money away from your event to use for bookkeeping.

Our nonprofit has never done a special event before and my board thought it would be fun to hire one of these 50's bands and sell the tickets as a way to raise money. I am not sure about this because we have to pay the band $25,000 up front whether we sell a ticket or not. What should I do?

This is a touchy situation because you want to respond to your board member's enthusiastic idea; however, this type of event puts the organization in debt immediately. And if no one buys a ticket, you will lose a lot of money. Ask 25 people (including board members and volunteers) to each make a gift of $1,000 to underwrite the event. This way, you won't have lost money on the event before you begin. You'll need more than $25,000—for invitations, tickets, flyers, and brochures; you may need to rent the hall or pay to put the performers up for the night. Whatever the total amount of the budget, ask your close friends and volunteers to underwrite the event and then sell tickets.

The chair of our special event this year wants to really do it up right and she can afford to put her own money into it to make it really special. Red flags are going off for me but I don't know why.

This is a bad precedent to set for your chair since it might imply that next year's chair should also be wealthy enough to put her own resources into the event and that will cause some hurt feelings on the part of those who want to chair but who cannot afford to fund an event. Here's a solution: Ask the chair to determine how much money she would like to earmark for the event, and then increase the event budget by that amount. This way the organization will know the true cost of the event and she will be able to have all the extras she wants.

Now where do I go?

BOOKS

Event Planning: The Ultimate Guide to Successful Meetings, Corporate Events, Fundraising Galas, Conferences, Conventions, Incentives, and Other Special Events
By Judy Allen
A comprehensive textbook about all aspects of special events. Includes sample worksheets.

The Business of Special Events: Fundraising Strategies for Changing Times
By A. Freedman, Harry A. and Karen Feldman
Directed at both experienced and novice event planners, provides practical advice and detailed checklists.

Special Events: Planning for Success
By April Harris
Offers many useful suggestions about planning a successful fundraising event. Geared primarily toward event planning at colleges and universities, but many of the suggestions apply to situations outside academia.

Successful Special Events: Planning, Hosting, and Evaluating
By Barbara R. Levy and Barbara H. Marion
Provides an overview of planning, hosting, and evaluating special events, giving special consideration to choice of theme and site, determination of cost, and time frame.

How to Produce Fabulous Fundraising Events: Reap Remarkable Returns with Minimal Effort
By Betty Stallings and Donna McMillion
Provides advice about choosing the right special event, selecting volunteers, planning, publicizing, and evaluating the event. Also contains a how-to guide for planning and managing a dinner event.

The Complete Guide to Fundraising Management
By Stanley Weinstein
Comprehensive treatment of fundraising principles and practices, including special events.

Special Events: Proven Strategies for Nonprofit Fund Raising
By Alan Wendroff
Provides a strategy for conducting special events, using the Master Event Timetable (METT) as a guide.

10
Writing a grant

the grant proposal

The top 10 things your grant proposal needs

Here's another way to fund your nonprofit programs: Get a grant. You can do it! You know your project cold. You know what you need to get it done. Your task: Tell donors all about it. And your first step is to write a **boilerplate**, or standardized, grant proposal. If you are good at multitasking, you can write your proposal and search for donors at the same time—but don't skimp on either task. They're both crucial.

If you've never seen a grant proposal before, you'll probably be surprised at how straightforward it is. Grant proposals consist of 10 basic sections, including supporting materials.

TIP: When you're writing your own boilerplate, approach the sections in the order listed here, with one exception: Save the introduction for last. You'll have a clearer idea of what to say once you've worked through the other sections. Use your case statement (see page 117) and organizing documents to bolster your grant.

- Introduction
  - Statement of Need
    - Goal
      - Objectives
        - Program Activities
          - Evaluation
            - History of the Organization and Its Funding
              - Summary or Conclusion
                - Project Budget
                  - Supporting Material
                    (résumé and press clippings)

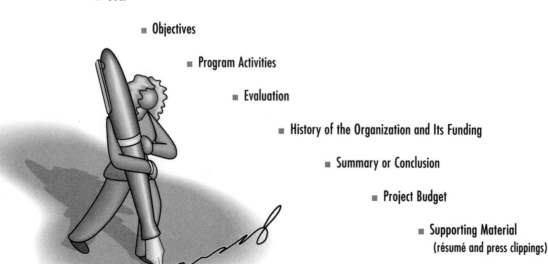

ASK THE EXPERTS

I have never written a grant proposal before, and I am worried that I won't be any good at it. What do I do?

Grant writing isn't all that hard, but it does mean entering into a new world with different rules and vocabulary. If you want a little help, consider taking a class on grant writing; your local college may offer such courses, and the Foundation Center conducts them all over the country. Check out its Web site (**www.fdncenter.org**) to learn more about when and where its grant-writing classes are held. Hospitals, colleges, and universities often have grantwriters on staff who might mentor you. Also, the Association of Fundraising Professionals (**www.afpnet.org**) may have a chapter near you. Ask for mentoring help.

The nonprofit organization I volunteer for needs a grant, and no one has the time to write a proposal. Can we hire a freelance grantwriter?

Sure. Many experienced grantwriters work on a freelance basis. You can find a list of them on the Foundation Center's Web site. You can also check with the American Association of Fundraising Counsel at 800-462-2372 or **www.aafrc.org** for information regarding freelance writers. Grantwriters usually charge by the proposal. A few charge a fee based on a percentage of the grant money obtained, but members of the Association of Fundraising Professionals oppose percentage-based rates because of ethical reasons. Be sure to find out the writer's track record before hiring; make sure the writer's experience matches the size and scope of your project.

Do I write a different proposal for each foundation I want to apply to?

Yes, but it's not as hard as it sounds. Once you have a basic boilerplate proposal in place, you edit it to address the needs and concerns of each prospective donor foundation.

The Name Game

When choosing a name for your project, remember; simple is best. It's fun to be cute and clever, but it's more important to be clear. Your project's name is the first contact people will have with your program. Keep it clear and informative. That way, it's more likely to attract interest.

Small Wonders
(Cute but obscure)

Helping Hand Child Care
(Clear and useful)

describing the need

The first step is to explain why the world needs your project. And when you make your statement of need (your description of the importance of your project), one rule reigns supreme: Be as specific as possible. Narrow down your statement of need as far as you can—the exact neighborhood, the precise age group, and other concrete descriptions. After reading this, a stranger should know exactly what problem you hope to set right, who will benefit, and where they are based.

But don't cram everything into this statement. You don't have to describe your project here. That comes later.

One trick that works well is to use statistics to support your statement of need. If children are lagging behind in school, cite area reading scores and compare them geographically. Look for any corroborating data such as demographic information, census numbers, and statistics. Any government studies in the area are especially helpful.

Another good way to underscore the need you describe is to quote a recognized source. Has a well-respected person spoken out against the problem? If so, add a short quote to your statement of need. Attachments are also helpful. Does a recent newspaper or magazine article describe the need you hope to address? Enclose a copy of any relevant clips with your proposal, and let them do some of the work for you.

TIP: Highlight the people you'll help, not your organization. It's not that your organization needs a new handicapped-access van. The need is that seven children who are developmentally disabled cannot go to the community park or school, because they have no safe, reliable transportation.

Statement of Need

When you're looking for information to support your statement of need, be sure to do your research thoroughly. Use the following criteria for choosing sources:

- **Be timely** Out-of-date information will undermine your credibility. Do your homework to make sure you have the very latest available statistics.

- **Be specific** If your program is in the Chicago area, focus your information hunt on Chicago. If you can, break it down by neighborhood. The more focused, the better.

- **Be brief** You'll make your case best by focusing on only one or two strong points.

Sample

Check out this sample statement of need. It establishes the need succinctly and with just enough detail to be compelling.

According to the governor's Annual Report on Primary Education, 57% of the children in Thursdon Hills cannot read at grade level at the end of their first school year. Yet the reading levels can be improved with tutoring support, which is not currently available to Thursdon Hills first graders. Martin Cary, director of the primary program at the state education department, says that reading scores can be improved by 30% to 60% if extra tutoring is given to children during the first grade.

what's your goal?

Let them know what you want to achieve

The next two steps in your proposal are similar, but not the same. A proposal's goal and its objectives belong together, and it helps to write them at the same time, but they are different in important ways.

The **goal** is a general statement. It's the outcome you hope for. It's a "vision thing," and that means it's short on detail. In fact, it's the shortest section in the whole proposal, because it must be clear enough to be expressed in a single sentence.

A good example of a goal is "to eliminate teen drug use in my neighborhood." It's hard to argue against it and also hard to see how you plan to do it. But the details belong in the next section: the objectives.

The **objectives** are a series of specific statements that fill in the details that the goal doesn't have. Most proposals include two or three concrete objectives for a program. They list the specific quantifiable ways you plan to reach your goal.

The main difference between your goal and your objectives is that goals cannot be measured and objectives can. In fact, your objectives can be measured so specifically that you will cite the dates and numbers you're aiming for.

It's easy to see how your goals and objectives are related, but they must work together to support the statement of need that opens your proposal. Make sure your objectives support your goals. Then make sure that both answer the need statement. If they do, congratulations. You're getting closer to winning your grant.

TIP: Use numbers or bullets to make your proposal easier to read.

Goal and Objectives

- Your goal is your final destination; your objectives are what you use to get there.

- The objectives specify how you intend to reach your goal.

Here and below are examples from a proposal for the hypothetical Growing Great Readers Project showing how these elements relate to each other.

Sample

This goal is a good general statement: It addresses a need that exists and is hard to argue against, but it does not say specifically how the need will be met.

The goal of the Growing Great Readers Project is to help first-grade children in Thursdon Hills become better readers.

Sample

Each objective is measurable: The comparative reading scores, the number of students, and the number of parents.

The objectives of the Growing Great Readers Project are:

- To offer a new after-school tutoring program aimed at improving reading scores for first graders at Thursdon Hills Elementary School.

- To enroll at least 50% of the first-grade children in the tutoring program. (The first graders number approximately 50 each fall.)

- To arrange for at least one parent of each child to attend a tutoring workshop to help support the child's reading efforts at home.

accomplishing your objectives

**The heart of
your proposal—
the program activities**

How do you plan to meet the objectives you've just outlined? Ah, there's the crucial question. And it's the program activities section in your proposal that needs to answer it.

Here you describe exactly what you plan to do. Explain how you will reach each of your objectives—and most important of all, keep your writing to the point. Describe your time frame, the activities you propose, and the staff (or volunteers) you'll require. Use a few relevant details, such as training your staff might need, any special supplies or equipment, and publicity. You needn't go into great detail here, but do mention items crucial for the success of the project.

A good way to help you organize your thoughts is to go through each of your objectives in order. Ask yourself, "What must be done in order to accomplish this objective?" List one to three activities needed to make it happen.

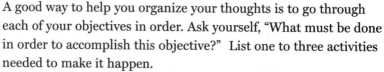

Who Will Staff Your Project?

Mention one or two major players here, no more. List names and relevant qualifications only. Refer to the rest of the staff by the categories in your budget: drivers, child-care aides, reading coaches, and so on.

Program Activities

In this section, describe the activities that will accomplish your project's objectives.

- Be specific.
- Include dates, schedules, and the titles of people involved in the work.

Sample

Note that the major activities are briefly listed and that they fulfill the three objectives for the project. The donor wants to know the basics of how the project will run, but without a lot of details.

At the beginning of August, a director with an MS in primary reading development will start the Growing Great Readers Project. She will talk with first-grade teachers at Thursdon Hills Elementary School in order to coordinate the project's tutoring program with the school's lesson plans. The director will train 30 volunteers from the Richardson Retirement Community.

Media releases and TV appearances by the director will advertise the Growing Great Readers Project in August and explain how the project can benefit all children. When parents come to register their first graders at the end of August, leaflets describing the tutoring sessions and the parent workshops will direct them to an enrollment desk. The director and volunteers will contact parents who do not enroll, explaining how the project can benefit each child.

During the school term, the first graders will meet with a trained volunteer twice a week after school to work on reading skills in the school cafeteria.

Three nights a week, the director will conduct repeat workshops to help parents hone their children's reading skills at home.

evaluating your project

How did you do?

Donors need to know that their money is being well spent. How will they know that? By having your project evaluated. Your proposal must include the way you will objectively measure how close you come to accomplishing the objectives you've stated. Sometimes that assessment is simple—an attendance tally, a collection of news clippings, or a report of lab results. Other times it may require summaries of reviews, user comments, or other, more complicated evaluations. And don't forget: If you need to pay for tests to measure your project's progress, make sure that expense is included in your budget. Meanwhile, most donors require periodic updates on projects, so prepare for a lot of letter writing.

FIRST PERSON INSIGHT

Delayed progress reports delay progress

When the school term ended, I suddenly realized I hadn't yet gotten around to sending in the quarterly results on our tutoring program for first-grade readers. I had just been so busy keeping everyone's schedule on target that I had forgotten all about it. I quickly pulled together the stats and sent a final report to our donor with a note apologizing for missing the midterm reports. To make things worse, the results for the year were merely okay, because seven students bused in from another district couldn't stay after school for tutoring. Then the donor program director told me he could have funded transportation for those kids had I only handed in my reports on time. I was dumbstruck. I'll never let a progress report slide again.

—Erica A., Houston, TX

Evaluation

This section explains how the effects of the Growing Great Readers Project will be measured and how the results will be communicated to the donor.

Sample

Each of the three objectives (page 169) is assigned a measurement.

During the first week of school, we will send a report on the number of students enrolled in the Growing Great Readers Project to the XYZ Foundation, as well as the number of parents who have signed up for the parent workshops. Attendance records for the tutoring sessions and the parent workshops will be forwarded at three-month intervals.

State when reports will be filed (in blue)

During the year, arrangements can be made for staff members from the XYZ Foundation to observe sessions in progress.

Tell how and when objectives will be measured

At the end of the school term, when the first-grade reading scores are released throughout the state, a complete report on the project will be submitted to the XYZ Foundation. The report will compare the Thursdon Hills Elementary School first-grade scores for the current year with those from the previous year.

Comparative ranking with other schools in the state will be analyzed. Summaries of reactions from both parents and teachers will also be included in the final report.

summing it up

Opening and closing

You're on the home stretch. There's only one more step to go. Actually, those are two more steps, but it's basically the same information written twice—once for the **introduction** and once for the **summary** or **conclusion** that appears at the end of the proposal.

Why did you have to save the intro for last? Well, you have to get through the other sections to have the best perspective on your project. Once you've written down all the details, you'll be able to write a more concise statement about the project as a whole. And the summary basically repeats the message of the introduction.

For better or worse, the introduction and summary are the most important parts of your proposal. Each section plays an important part, but the introduction and the summary are crucial. Program officers at donor foundations are very busy, and they may not read all parts of every proposal that crosses their desks. They often decide whether to proceed based on the introduction or summary. Make these steps clear and precise so your proposal passes to the next level.

Introduction

In a paragraph, state who you are, what the problem is, how you propose to fix it—and your organization's qualifications for the job. Begin by reading over the sections you have already written. Mention the amount of money you want, and be sure to work in the name of the donor you are applying to. Make it straightforward. Try to use action verbs to make it sound lively. For instance:

Sample

> The reading test scores of children in Graham County are nearly the lowest in the state. To improve performance, the Parent Teacher Association of Thursdon Hills Elementary School is establishing an educational project called Growing Great Readers. With support from the XYZ Foundation in the amount of $45,000, we will create a tutorial program in which volunteers from the local retirement home will help to improve the reading scores of our first graders.

Summary

In closing, sum up what you have said in the proposal. It will be similar to the introduction, but express it in different words. Add a warm, somewhat emotional appeal. Try to give the prospective donor a reason for helping you with your project.

Sample

> With the generous help of the XYZ Foundation in the amount of $45,000, we will address the substandard reading performance of the children of the Thursdon Hills Elementary School with our Growing Great Readers Project. We will train volunteer tutors to coach our first graders in a way that will enhance the teachers' efforts. We will advise our parents on how to enrich their children's reading experiences at home. These projects will allow our students to establish a sound foundation in reading skills and enable them to perform more consistently in every subject throughout their school years.

supporting material

Show how much support you already have

Writing a grant is a bit like applying for a job—you want to put your best foot forward. How do you do that? Well, just as you would do for a job, get letters of recommendation. And be sure to ask for them early—it can take time for people to write them.

Start with your local political leaders. Ask your mayor or the president of your town council to write a letter endorsing your project and your nonprofit organization. You want them to help you make a case for your project. If you can, get letters of endorsement from your congressperson and senator.

Once you have a letter of support from a civic leader, ask for letters of endorsement from those who would be affected by your project. For example, if your project is to fund a middle school reading program, ask for letters of support from the board of education and the superintendent of schools. A few earnest letters from middle school teachers might be important, too.

Ideally, your nonprofit organization has garnered a few press clippings about its work. Collect those in a file, then see which ones are relevant to your proposal. Make copies of these to include with it. Also, consider press stories that underscore the need for your project. For instance, an article alerting readers to the increasing rate of teenage drug use in your town would be ideal to include with a proposal for a project designed to help teens stay off drugs.

Next consider the people who will be working on the project once it gets funded. If any have impressive academic or professional credentials, get copies of their résumés. You will want to send them out with your proposal.

The final piece of paper you will need to get is a copy of your nonprofit or nonprofit sponsor's 501(c)(3) IRS tax-exempt letter.

ASK THE EXPERTS

How many letters of recommendation should I get?

You really need only two, possibly three. You don't want to flood your proposal with a slew of letters. The point you want to make is that you have community backing for your project.

I am still waiting for a letter of endorsement from my congresswoman. How long does it take to write one of these letters?

It doesn't take long to write them, but it may take a while to get the ball rolling. You can help things along in your request with a few tricks: Include key points about your project so that she can write about them. And give a deadline for when you need a reply. If it's clear you are not going to get a letter from one civic leader, move on to another. For this reason, it's always good to ask several people for letters. It's better to get more than you need and pick out the best ones for submission.

Can I offer to write the letter of recommendation and have the person sign it?

Yes, you can. To speed the process along, it is helpful to write a generic sample letter of endorsement about your project and mail, fax, or e-mail it to prospective endorsers. Tactfully, tell them they are welcome to use your exact words or pick and choose phrases and paragraphs as they see fit. Remind them to use their own letterhead and provide an original signature.

TIP: A letter from someone who has used your service often has the highest impact. If a parent or child sends you a note, ask for written permission to use it, then copy it. Don't retype or edit it. Use their thankful voice without interpretation. Let those who you've helped tell your story.

the budget summary

Budgets are important. Really important. Foundations want to see that you have done your homework and know exactly the amount of money your project will need. And they will reject grants with unrealistic budgets immediately. So you may want to leave this part to a financial professional in the organization—the tax lawyer or accountant. If there is no such warm body, then you'll have to do it. First, set up some meetings with the key people involved and get their financial input. You'll also need to include budgetary information on your nonprofit sponsor. Meanwhile, here's what's likely to be included in most project budget summaries.

A list of your expenses

- **Salaries and wages** If your proposal calls for hiring someone, indicate whether the position is full- or part-time, and don't forget benefits and payroll tax. Also list any expenses needed for training.

- **Travel, equipment, printing, and copying** Try to estimate these costs as accurately as you can.

- **Rent and utilities** These amounts are usually fixed.

A list of your revenue

- **Other grants** List any that you have already secured from other funders.

- **Individual donations**

- **Fundraising events and products**

- **In-kind support** These are donated goods and services that will help support your project. Find the estimated value of volunteer time at **www.independentsector.org** ($16.00 an hour in 2006).

TIP: The difference between your expenses and revenue is the amount you are seeking to be covered by grants. Do not ask one donor to fund your entire project. Instead, ask several donors to fund various parts of your budget; for example, staffing or utilities.

To give you an idea about the possible items to list in your expenses and revenue columns, use this budget summary from the common grant application of the National Network of Grantmakers. Find it at www.nng.org. (For more information on the common grant application, see page 181.)

IV. BUDGET

If you already prepare organizational and project budgets that approximate this format, please feel free to submit them in their original forms. You may reproduce this form on your computer and/or submit separate pages for income and expenses.

Budget for the period: _____ to _____

EXPENSES			INCOME	
Item	Amount	FT/PT	Source	Amount
Salaries & wages (break down by individual position and indicate full- or part-time)	$_____	_____	Government grants & contracts (specify)	$_____
	_____	_____		
	_____	_____		
	_____	_____	Foundations (specify)	$_____
	_____	_____	Corporations	$_____
	_____	_____	Religious institutions	$_____
Fringe benefits & payroll taxes	$_____		United Way/Combined Federal Campaign & other federated campaigns	$_____
Consultants & professional fees	$_____			
Travel	$_____		Individual contributions	$_____
Equipment	$_____		Fundraising events & products	$_____
Supplies	$_____			
Training	$_____		Membership income	$_____
Printing & copying	$_____		In-kind support	$_____
Telephone & fax	$_____		Other (earned income, consulting fees, etc. Please specify.)	$_____
Postage & delivery	$_____			
Rent & utilities	$_____		_____	_____
In-kind expense	$_____		_____	_____
Other (specify)	$_____		_____	_____
_____				
TOTAL EXPENSE	$_____		TOTAL INCOME	$_____
			BALANCE	$_____

a grant template

Grant proposals online

If it all seems overwhelming and you can't organize your thoughts, don't panic. Help is at hand from several excellent templates that you can use to help organize your writing. They are known as **common grant applications**, and you can download them onto your computer.

One of the more useful ones was created by the National Network of Grantmakers, a group of more than 50 donors who share common philanthropic interests. Their application includes fill-in-the-blank forms for a cover sheet and budget, a narrative outline, and an attachments checklist. This can help you write a more cohesive proposal, and it's a standard form for applying to any of the donors in the network. (Think of it as a common application form for all the colleges on the East Coast—that's how valuable it is to grant seekers.) Check out their common grant application online at **www.nng.org**, and choose "common grant application."

You can check an index of other common grant applications at **www.fdncenter.org**. Click on Finding Funders, then click on Common Grant Applications. (This will take you to the long Web address **fdncenter.org/funders/cga/index.html**.) Use the list to obtain common forms, to find out if a donor you are targeting uses a common format, and to find other like-minded donors who accept the same format.

On the opposite page is a sample checklist for attachments from the common grant application created by the National Network of Grantmakers.

III. ATTACHMENTS/REQUIREMENTS (Supply everything checked below by funder who prepared this copy.)

A. Evaluation

☐ 1. Briefly describe your plan for evaluating the success of the project or for your organization's work. What questions will be addressed? Who will be involved in evaluating this work—staff, board, constituents, community, consultants? How will the evaluation results be used?

B. Organizational Structure/Administration

☐ 1. Briefly describe how your organization works: What are the responsibilities of board, staff and volunteers?
And if membership organization, define criteria for membership. Are there dues?
☐ 2. Who will be involved in carrying out the plans outlined in this request? Include a brief paragraph summarizing the qualifications of key individuals involved.
☐ 3. Provide a list of your board of directors with related demographic information.
☐ 4. How is the board selected, who selects them and how often?
☐ 5. Include an organizational chart showing decision-making structure.

C. Finances

☐ 1. Most recent, completed full year organizational financial statement (expenses, revenue and balance sheet), audited, if available.
☐ 2. Organization's current annual operating budget (See attached budget format).
☐ 3. Current project budget, other than general support (See attached format).
☐ 4. Projected operating budget for upcoming year (See attached format).
☐ 5. List individually other funding sources for this request. Include amounts and whether received, committed or projected/pending.
☐ 6. Describe your plans for future fund raising.
☐ 7. A copy of your IRS 501(c)(3) letter. If you do not have 510(c)(3) status, check with the funder to see if they are willing to fund through your fiscal sponsor or are willing to exercise expenditure responsibility. Additional information may be required to do so.
☐ 8. Other

D. Other Supporting Material

☐ 1. Letters of support/commitment (up to three).
☐ 2. Recent newsletter articles, newspaper clippings, evaluations or reviews (up to three).
☐ 3. Recent annual report.
☐ 4. Videos/cassettes are accepted ONLY if this box is checked.
☐ 5. Other

Guidelines for applicants (completed by funder)

Send ___ number of complete copies: cover sheet, five page proposal and attachments that are checked off.

Use a standard typeface no smaller than 10 points and no less than .25 in margins .

Proposals by fax are ☐ are not ☐ accepted.

Binders or folders are ☐ are not ☐ accepted.

Your proposal must be ☐ double sided ☐ single sided ☐ no preference.

Please use the following paper ☐ white/very light colored, ☐ recycled,
                              ☐ 8½ x 11 inches only, ☐ no preference.

Sí, aceptamos las solicitudes de fondos en español . ☐ Yes, we accept funding proposals in Spanish.
No aceptamos las solicitudes en español. ☐ No, we do not accept funding proposals in Spanish.

Funder who prepared this copy of the Common Grant Application: _____

now what do I do?
Answers to common questions

Several foundations have sent me application forms to fill out in lieu of writing proposals. Should I skip writing out a boilerplate proposal?

You can, but that's not something an expert would advise you to do. The process of writing a proposal will help you think through your project from a funder's point of view. And there's another benefit: You can also use sections from your basic proposal to fill in the application forms that some foundations require. Chances are, if your application is accepted, the funder will want to see more information, in which case you will send off your tailored boilerplate proposal.

I don't type well. Can I write my proposal neatly by hand?

Draft your proposal however you work best, but be prepared to have it typed by someone. You cannot submit handwritten proposals.

I still don't see how to tell the goal from the objectives. Aren't they all the same thing in different words?

No. Each is different. The goal is the overall aim of your project (a lunch program for summer campers). The objectives tell the specific measures to be used to achieve that aim (recruiting five volunteers to make lunch one day a week for four weeks).

What if our grant project runs into unexpected expenses?

If legitimate unforeseen expenses crop up, be sure to go back to the donor or grantmaker and inform them of the situation. If they seem sensitive to the turn of events, then ask for more money. If they don't have the funds, they may be able to steer you toward someone who does. Foundations tend to know each other's situations and interests. An inside recommendation is a great tip.

Now where do I go?

CONTACTS

The Independent Sector
www.independentsector.org
This Web site is the membership site for major charities

The North Carolina Center for Nonprofits
www.ncnonprofits.org
This Web Site acts as a clearinghouse for the nonprofits in North Carolina.

www.fdncenter.org/learn/shortcourse/ prop1.html
Proposal writing

nonprofit.miningco.com/msubgra.htm
Proposal writing

Grantsmanship Center
www.tgci.com

Association of Small Foundations
www.smallfoundations.org

BOOKS

The Foundation Center's Guide to Proposal Writing
By Jane C. Geever and Patricia McNeill

Secrets of Successful Grantsmanship: A Guerrilla Guide to Raising Money
By Susan L. Golden

Proposal Planning and Writing
By Jerry Griffith and Lynne E. Miner

Grantseeking: A Basic Step-by-Step Approach
By Lehman Zimmerman and Associates

Finding Funding: Grantwriting from Start to Finish Including Project Management and Internet Use
Edited by Ernest W. Brewer, Charles Achilles, Jay R. Fuhrimann, and Connie Hollingsworth

The Complete Guide to Getting a Grant: How to Turn Your Ideas into Dollars
By Laurie Blum

11
Going forward

getting bigger

Define your growing needs

You did it! You started a nonprofit, and it is meeting the needs of the community. Congratulations! But chances are, the needs you are meeting are growing. You have two options: Stay as you are—a small nonprofit that relies predominantly on volunteers to get the work done—or grow your nonprofit. This means raising more money and hiring staff. In short, making your nonprofit function more like a for-profit business. While this may sound daunting, it is very manageable if you take it in small steps.

For most nonprofits, hiring paid staff is the hardest hurdle to overcome. One reason is that most start-up nonprofits haven't had the luxury of having the right people for the right job. In fact, most start-ups are not even aware of what specific skills they need. That's why your first order of business is to have a board meeting and discuss what those specific needs are and then write job descriptions that match those needs. Do not think in terms of title, but rather in terms of function. Then determine the salary you think matches the job description.

Next consider salary. Do you want to hire experienced employees who can hit the ground running and fulfill those job functions immediately? Or would you prefer to hire inexperienced people and train them in how you like things done? The former will save time; the latter will save money. Discuss with your board which way you want to go.

ASK THE EXPERTS

A few of our volunteers are upset about having to hire staff members. How can I reassure them?

Change is always hard. As an organization grows, its history can be lost or take on a dimmer gleam as new workers are brought in. Before you hire anyone, have a meeting with your volunteers and explain the changes you are undertaking. Explain how new people will make your mission that much more effective. Ask for their input in writing job descriptions. Or ask them to research how other community nonprofits work.

Writing a Job Description

■ List the key responsibilities in this job. Start each function with an active verb; for example, answer the phone, file letters, write donor thank-you cards, represent your nonprofit at town meetings.

■ Next describe the desired outcome you want to have when each of those job functions is being met; for example, a more ordered office; donor satisfaction; greater presence in the community.

■ Match those functions to a title and then determine the level of experience you want with the salary you can afford.

hiring paid staff

What to look for
when hiring staff

The good news is that once you have written the job description, you can use it as your advertisement for the job. When the résumés start coming in, don't be tempted to hire the first person who answers the ad. A lot of startups are so short of help that they often offer the job to the first person who answers the ad whether he or she fits the job or not. So take your time and wait until you get a handful of résumés and then interview each one by telephone first, then see the few finalists in person.

The candidate you want will not only have the right skills but also the right fit. That means asking questions that reveal the right skills and the right personality.

Personality-Revealing Questions:

■ **How do others describe you?** Ask candidates for specific situations in which they demonstrated those qualities.

■ **What are your long-term career goals?** This question will flesh out how candidates view this current job, as well as their hopes for future employment.

■ **In which areas would your most respected critic say you need improvement?** Here you want candidates to reveal any shortcomings they see in themselves.

In addition to personality questions, you also want to ask questions that reveal how a candidate will behave or act on the job. To do that, you need to draw on the candidate's past experiences.

10 Great Behavior-Based Interview Questions

1. Describe a situation where you had a conflict with someone and how you handled it successfully.

2. Tell me about a time when you increased productivity or improved operations.

3. What is the one thing you would want to improve at your former job, and how would you do it?

4. Tell me about a time when you gave exceptional client service.

5. Describe a time when you had to juggle several tasks at one time and how you prioritized your work.

6. Give me an example of a situation where you had to exert leadership to get the job done. How do you define leadership?

7. Tell me about a time when you needed to change your personal style of work in order to work with people who were different from you.

8. What are the skills you still need to acquire in order to advance in your career?

9. Of all the people you have worked for, who did you enjoy working for the most and why?

10. What is the most useful criticism you have ever received?

creating a for-profit adjunct business

Raising money the for-profit way

Going from a start-up to a thriving nonprofit requires new ways of fundraising. In today's world, there is greater competition for donor dollars. And now for-profits have started to enter into the nonprofit domain. You might want to consider joining their ranks.

One way to add to your funding is to start a for-profit venture to support your nonprofit business. You may have already come up against for-profit issues if your nonprofit earned money that was not related to the nonprofit. For example, if your nonprofit owned an apartment building, the IRS would absolutely tax you on that income. That tax is called Unrelated Business Income Tax (UBIT). (In fact, the IRS has a special form for nonprofits to report any UBIT, see page 95 for more.)

If you want to start a for-profit business that will not be subject to federal income tax, then the IRS will have to determine if your for-profit business is related to your nonprofit business or not. Nonprofit is really a misnomer—nonprofits do make a profit, and it is perfectly legal and acceptable for one not to be taxed. The reason

why this is all right is that nonprofits do not have stockholders, so any "profit" they make can be left in a savings account or put in an endowment fund or used to pay the nonprofit's bills or to expand its programs.

Social Entrepreneurship

A healthy nonprofit organization needs diversified sources of funding; for example, from individual donors, foundations, corporations, and governments. But given recent cutbacks, nonprofits are starting earned-income ventures where they generate profits, which, in turn, are spent on improving the nonprofit's services to the community.

This earned income is being called social entrepreneurship. A word of caution about starting a for-profit venture. If it grows too quickly and becomes a substantial part of your nonprofit, you can lose your 501(c)(3) exempt status. One solution is to start a for-profit subsidiary, which your nonprofit may or may not control, and transfer all your unrelated business activity to it. That way you keep the two businesses separate. Be sure to check with your accountant before you start a for-profit.

Another potential problem is that the mission of your nonprofit may get lost as it grows. For this reason, a number of nonprofits today are spending lots of money on consultants who are helping them write value statements as well as mission statements. A value statement clearly identifies the hallmarks of behavior or service that will be cherished and rewarded within the organization.

merging with another nonprofit

Doubling your mission

Merging with another nonprofit organization can be the best way to utilize your nonprofit's resources. The most common reason for a merger is that the community cannot support both organizations. If there is another organization in town that does work similar to yours, or is providing different services to the same populations, this can create confusion among donors, as well as among those whom you are trying to serve. In the end, neither of you can flourish. In this case, it may be a great idea to merge the two organizations.

This type of merger not only clears away the confusion but provides an economy of scale. By joining services, you can cut down on overhead expenses and have more money for your programs.

But just like for-profit businesses, nonprofits have cultures, histories, and ways of doing things. The merger of two organizations can be difficult if these differences and the idiosyncrasies of each aren't acknowledged or given reverence.

Two Boards of Directors

How do you merge the two boards of directors along with the CEO of both organizations? You both need to meet to lay out your ideas, your long-range views and plans, and to discuss what you are willing to take on and willing to give up. There will be change. It can be managed well by thinking it through, talking it over, and sticking to the joint implementation plan. But if one ego or personality is going to make its mark in the process, the merger will hurt many paid and unpaid staff people who were and are dedicated to the two old organizations.

shutting down your nonprofit

When it's time to stop

Most nonprofits do not go out of business, but rather they change their mission or expand their areas of operation. This often happens when founders leave the start-up. Ideally, the new mission will generate the same excitement as the old one. But if it doesn't, it is time to consider shutting down.

How do you shut down? First, check your bylaws for your guidelines as to what is supposed to happen to the organization's assets when and if the organization ever ends. You must do what you said you would do. Whether you sell the assets and the cash is turned over to the Community Foundation or United Way or whether it is distributed in some other way, you must follow your bylaws. Second, you need to create an organization-wide plan for how and when you will shut down and how you will tell your paid staff, volunteers, and donors.

Most states require that you notify the secretary of state to communicate your plan. All the contracts need to be dissolved or bought out, the rent paid to the end of the month, the furniture sold or given to another nonprofit, the final 990 or tax forms filed, and the key placed under the flower pot by the front door.

Whatever you do, don't close without celebrating all that you were able to contribute. This is important so that your volunteers and staff can feel good about what they achieved. It will also add credibility to those whom you served that they may share in the rejoicing that their lives were changed or the problem was solved.

ASK THE EXPERTS

Our founder moved, and we have found that without her our nonprofit is floundering. Should we shut down?

It is common for a nonprofit that "loses" its founder to flounder, lose its compass, and wonder if it should close or change course. There is no right answer. The questions are:

- Is our mission still relevant?

- If not, how can we change it in order to better meet current and future needs?

- If so, what new programs can we add to revitalize the organization?

- What new markets can we tap into that might want to take part in our organization?

- What new revenue streams can we access?

- What new volunteers can we recruit to make our new future even more exciting?

TIP: If the volunteers in your nonprofit are too tired, discouraged, or downright hostile or negative, it might be time to close the organization gracefully.

now what do I do?
Answers to common questions

What questions can't I ask during a job interview?

In a job interview, you should stay away from asking questions of a personal nature. They are not relevant to the job. You are interviewing to see if the candidate's skills and talents match the skills and talents needed to do the job. Be clear on what personality characteristics are required to make the office and team work at their maximum efficiency and ability. Whether the candidate is married, has children, is of a certain faith, or prefers a certain lifestyle is not your business and not the candidate's business to bring into the office.

How often should we do personnel reviews? We are all working for practically no money, and I feel bad doing this.

If you are uncomfortable helping people review their annual goals and achievements, fake it 'til you make it! Annual reviews (if not semiannual) of goals or outcomes are essential for the funders who support you. They need to know that someone (and you are the chief) is holding staff members accountable for their work, no matter how low the salaries.

How do I fire a staff member, a board member, and a volunteer?

The answer is almost the same for all three. If you start with clear expectations that are written down and agreed to by the volunteer or staff member, it is easier to look at that document and compare the person's performance against it. That document should contain a list of the consequences if certain provisions are violated. For example, if you work in a human service or medical organization, there are strict requirements—in fact, legal requirements—about confidentiality. So when a staff member is hired or a board member is elected or a volunteer begins to serve, he is going to be held accountable for keeping his mouth closed about confidential business. If he violates this trust, you must take action; whether a verbal warning, suspension without pay for a day, or immediate firing and removal of that person from the premises. If you list the consequences of violations up front, and the other person signs the statement admitting that he understands the consequences, it is much easier to fire him.

We are planning on shutting our doors, and we have some assets left to distribute. Who decides who should get this money?

The current board of directors makes the decision as to where the money should go. Experts recommend that the recipient organization be of a like kind to yours that is a federally recognized 501 (c) (3).

Our organization has merged with another nonprofit and moved offices. What should I do with all the plaques thanking former donors?

In the new organization it is important to honor those who gave their money to the former organization. Hang the plaques in a place of honor so all can see the generations of support your organization has received and continues to receive.

Now where do I go?

BOOKS

Venture Forth! The Essential Guide to Starting a Moneymaking Business in Your Nonprofit Organization
By Rolfe Larson

Coping with Cutbacks: The Nonprofit Guide to Success When Times Are Tight
By Emil Angelica and Vincent Hyman

glossary

501 (c) (3) A classification awarded by the IRS designating a certain type of charitable organization as a nonprofit, tax-exempt operation. There are other classes of nonprofits.

1023 The form to be completed by the organization in order to apply for nonprofit status from the Internal Revenue Service.

990 The form to be filed annually with the Internal Revenue Service showing the financial operations of the nonprofit.

Advisory board A group of well-meaning, like-minded individuals who come together to give their advice and input for the benefit of a specific organization. Advisers are not legally responsible for the governance of the organization. They are friends or ambassadors for the organization.

Annual plan An annual plan describes the specific outcomes that the organization plans to achieve within the calendar year, its fiscal year or within a specified 12-month period. It includes a budget of income and expenses, and the paid and unpaid staffing resources needed to fulfill the plan.

Annual report This document states in numbers, words, and pictures the organization's activities for a 12-month period. The annual report is used to inform donors, volunteers, and service users what was accomplished by the organization.

Audit A review and report done by professional certified public accountants, usually on an annual or biannual basis, which examines not only the financial status of the organization but also the processes by which money and contributions are received, processed, and paid out.

Board of directors The board is the governing group of volunteers responsible for the organization. The board does not receive payment for services; in fact, they are usually expected to make financial contributions to the welfare of the organization. The board is the legal entity for the nonprofit organization and meets to oversee the fiscal and operational health of the organization and ensure that the organization's mission is being faithfully implemented through quality programs. It hires, evaluates, and when necessary fires the Executive Director.

Board of trustees *See* Board of directors.

Bylaws The set of rules or guidelines by which an organization will operate. Bylaws spell out the terms of office for directors, for the officers, define the fiscal year dates, and specify what will happen to the organization's assets should it fold, merge, or change in some way.

Case for support A document that describes in a complete way the supportable nature of the organization, project by project or department by department. The case for support is updated annually, is long and thorough, and has all the relevant supplemental information someone might need when writing a grant proposal or solicitation letter.

Case statement A document that states clearly, completely, and passionately the need for contributed funds for a specific project. Usually it has photographs, explanatory captions, charts, or graphs and is an eye-catching document limited in length.

Charitable gift receipt *See* tax receipt.

Coalition A relationship between two or more organizations or individuals who marshal resources and pool them to achieve a common goal. Usually the purpose is a broad but single issue, such as a coalition to fight hunger, or to eradicate HIV-AIDS.

Collaboration A relationship between two or more organizations or individuals. Usually coalitions are short term and single-issue focused.

Corporation A legal entity that has a charter registered by the state which creates it.

Development plan The detailed fundraising plan that shows the activities to be undertaken in a 12-month period to attract donations of cash, grants, pledges, and in-kind contributions to support the operations, programs, buildings, and grounds through an endowment (or long-term savings) of the organization.

EIN Employer Identification Number; assigned by the federal government to organizations that employ workers. It is required before an organization can ask for special tax status.

Evaluation A process of comparing what actually happened with what was expected in order to see if goals were achieved, actions fell short, or were above expectations. Evaluations are usually done on an annual basis (unless otherwise stated) and are done on employees, volunteers, board members as well as programs and departments.

Executive director *See* Board of directors.

External case *See* Case statement.

For profit A business, company, corporation or organization that has a board of directors, stockholders, and shares.

Fundraising plan *See* Development plan.

Goal An achievable action that is broad in nature.

Grant A charitable gift from a foundation, government, or business that is usually very specifically applied for, with rules and regulations about how it must be spent. Grants can be one-time or for a period of up to three years. Grants usually have guidelines to help people apply for them.

Incorporating A process that a group of people go through in order to gain a legal status for a business that will become a nonprofit or for-profit organization.

In-kind contribution A gift of time, advice, things, space, equipment, or other tangible property that is not cash or immediately liquid.

Internal case *See* Case for support.

Letter of exemption An official statement from the Internal Revenue Service granting a temporary or permanent tax status that allows charitable contributions to be treated in a way different for the donors.

Long-range plan, Long-term plan *See* Strategic plan.

Marketing plan Usually also known as a communications plan, this lists all the communications activities the organization will undertake in order to attract service users, donors, volunteers, and board members. It also states how various market segments will be communicated with, when, and through what techniques. It lays out an orchestrated plan of action for a 12-month period that corresponds with the operation's plan.

NGO Nongovernmental organization. Usually refers to a European nonprofit.

Nonprofit Term used to describe a not-for-profit organization. It is misleading because not for profits can earn or make a profit and keep the money.

Not for profit Correct terminology for an organization that has been designated to receive tax-deductible contributions.

NPO Nonprofit organization. The new terminology in the nonprofit sector.

Objective An achievable action that is specific in nature and has a time deadline associated with it.

Operating plan A plan with very specific detail regarding who will provide what functions on a week-to-week basis (if not a day-to-day basis). The operating plan shows who reports to whom, how the activities of the organization will be carried out, how decisions will be made and implemented, and how much each activity will cost and be paid for. The operating plan is like a specific step-by-step playbook so that all the paid and unpaid staff can work in partnership toward the same goals.

Organization chart A visual map of job positions and the authority and supervisory responsibilities within the organization. An organization chart speaks in general terms of positions (no personal names are used) and includes paid and volunteer staff and leaders, including the board of directors.

Pledge A promise for a charitable contribution that will be paid by a specific date. Often pledges are larger than a single gift size, multiplied by the number of years over which the pledge payment is to be made.

Section 509 (a)(3) Supporting Organizations Supporting organizations are public charities that carry out their exempt purposes by supporting one or more other exempt organizations, usually other public charities. The category can cover many types of entities, including university endowment funds and organizations that provide essential services for hospital systems. The classification is important because it is one means by which a charity can avoid classification as a private foundation, a status that is subject to a much more restrictive regulatory regimen. The key feature of a supporting organization is a strong relationship with an organization it supports. This relationship enables the supported organization to oversee the operations of the supporting organization. Therefore, the supporting organization is classified as a public charity, even though it may be funded by a small number of persons in a manner that is similar to a private foundation.

SS-4 The IRS application for an employer identification number that you will need in order to open a checking and savings account for your nonprofit.

Strategic plan A plan usually of a long length of time and broad in perspective in order to examine the strengths and weaknesses of the organization, economic opportunities projected and economic and social threats to it as determined by a specific group of paid or unpaid staff people. The advantage of having a strategic plan (also known as a long-term plan) is that it states the projected economic and social expectations for a future time period that will affect (positively or negatively) the organization. If any of these assumptions changes, the plan can be adjusted for the new expectations.

Task list A regularly produced document that states the actions each individual is to achieve by specific dates. The list has every participant's name on it and lists every task so there can be no confusion about who is taking what action or by what time.

Tax-exempt number Government entities are frequently asked to provide a tax-exempt number or "determination" letter to prove status as a "tax-exempt" or charitable entity. For example, applications for grants from a private foundation or a charitable organization generally require this information as part of the application process. In addition, donors frequently ask for this information as substantiation that the donor's contribution is tax deductible, and vendors may ask for this to substantiate that the organization is exempt from sales or excise taxes.

There is no tax-exempt number provided by the Internal Revenue Service. A government entity may use its federal TIN (taxpayer identification number), also referred to as an EIN (Employer Identification Number), for identification purposes.

Tax receipt A receipt generated by a not-for-profit organization to a donor specifying the amount of a gift, the form it took (such as cash, credit card, stock) the date it was received, the pledge amount and payments toward it (if applicable) and the purpose to which the gift will be applied if so specified by the donor. It is legally required that gifts in the amount of $250 or more must be acknowledged with a receipt to the donor, but it is a good habit for all gifts to be acknowledged in this way.

index

about the author

Ann Fritschner is an advanced certified professional fundraiser and a long-time member of the Association of Fundraising Professionals. In her seminars, Ann trains nonprofit staff members on the art and science of raising money as well as how to attract productive volunteers and board members. She teaches at the Duke University Center for Nonprofit Management. She is also an ordained deacon in the Episcopal Church and is a chaplain at a church for the homeless in Asheville, NC.

Barnes & Noble Basics
Barbara J. Morgan Publisher
Barb Chintz Editorial Director
Leonard Vigliarolo Design Director
Gina Graham Editorial Assistant
Della R. Mancuso Production Manager
James Trimarco Design Assistant

Barnes & Noble Books would like to thank the following consultants for their help in preparing this book:
Alexia Jurschak, of the Katonah Village Improvement Society, Katonah, NY, and
Wayne Henry, a partner in the Omaha office of Stinson Morrison Hecker LLP.